AN INTRODUCTION TO CRYSTAL GRIDS

AN INTRODUCTION TO
CRYSTAL GRIDS

DAILY RITUALS FOR YOUR
HEART, HEALTH, AND HAPPINESS

Karen Frazier

**ROCKRIDGE
PRESS**

For Tristan

For general information on our other products and services or to obtain technical support, please contact our Customer Care Department within the U.S. at (866) 744-2665, or outside the U.S. at (510) 253-0500.

Rockridge Press publishes its books in a variety of electronic and print formats. Some content that appears in print may not be available in electronic books, and vice versa.

TRADEMARKS: Rockridge Press and the Rockridge Press logo are trademarks or registered trademarks of Callisto Media Inc. and/or its affiliates, in the United States and other countries, and may not be used without written permission. All other trademarks are the property of their respective owners. Rockridge Press is not associated with any product or vendor mentioned in this book.

Interior and Cover Designer: Rachel Haeseker
Photo Art Director/Art Manager: Sue Smith
Editor: Carolyn Abate
Production Editor: Ashley Polikoff
Production Manager: Riley Hoffman
Cover photograph: © Serena Williamson/iStock
Interior photography: © Shutterstock and © iStock
Author photo courtesy of Karen Frazier

ISBN: Print 978-1-64611-066-7 | eBook 978-1-64611-067-4

Ro

CONTENTS

INTRODUCTION

Often I get the same phone call, text, DM, or private conversation. Sometimes from friends—and sometimes even from complete strangers. The words and delivery method may vary, but the context is remarkably similar.

"I just bought _____ crystal. I blame you."

I get it, and I gladly accept the blame. Crystals are cool, and I can't help but share my love for them with others through my teaching and writing. Crystals have brought so much good into my life that I want to show people the amazing things they can do for us and for the energy of our planet and the universe we inhabit.

I believe crystals are conscious entities that come from the planet, vibrating not only with Earth energy but also with the pure intention and unconditional love of the universe. Crystals come into our lives when we need them to help us learn, grow, and expand on our journeys as light beings living in human bodies.

Crystals are pathfinders and guides; lodestars that clarify our path and allow us to better flow with the plan the universe has for us. They can help us clear blocked energy, balance uneven energy flow, amplify positive juju, and release or transmute negative vibes. Through crystals we can better hear messages from our higher selves, our spirit guides, and more. Crystals allow us not only to receive positive energy but also share powerful and harmonious vibrational frequencies with fellow travelers in this universe.

When brought together synergistically and arranged in sacred geometric shapes that magnify their vibrational potential, these beautiful stones become exponentially more than the sum of their parts. Just imagine the collective vibrations of multiple crystals arranged in an intentional way. That is the power of a crystal grid. They are creative, beautiful, and provide potent, directed energy.

One of my favorite places to utilize crystal grids is in my classroom when I teach. These "learning grids" help me communicate the information my students need the most while also helping them be receptive to that information. I'm a fan of creating grids in my bedroom, too, because they help channel Divine guidance in dreams and spark inspiration in my writing, making the words flow effortlessly.

As I write this, I have a crystal grid set up nearby. As you're about to learn, crystal grids can facilitate the flow of energy in your life as you walk your own path and serve the universe in your own unique and beautiful way.

PART 1

GETTING STARTED WITH CRYSTAL GRIDS

CHAPTER 1

The Power of Crystal Grids

WHENEVER TWO OR MORE high-vibration objects are used together, each magnifies the other, making the combination even more powerful. This effect sums up the potential of crystal grids. Using one crystal is a dynamic way to increase vibration and focus your intention. When you combine them to create sacred geometric shapes, as in a crystal grid, that potency is magnified, and the focus is refined, expanded, or both.

WHAT CRYSTAL GRIDS CAN DO FOR YOU

Working with crystal grids is a creative and intuitive pursuit. For inspiration, you can use the grids in this book or patterns you might discover elsewhere. Once you understand the effects of combining multiple crystals with the intention and meaning behind sacred geometry, you can start to build your own grids specifically focused on your personal intentions. The guidelines and suggested layouts in this book are a starting point. If you feel guided to try something different, trust your intuition. Feel free to find the freedom in working with crystal grids in a manner that is meaningful to you.

The dynamic pairing of multiple crystals and meaningful geometric shapes—combined with your focus and intent—can help you manifest and expand energy in the most significant aspects of your life, serving your highest and greatest good.

WELLNESS

Just as you can work with single crystals to influence the wellness of your body, mind, and spirit, a crystal grid can help amplify healing. Often illnesses and conditions arise from a confluence of various physical, mental, emotional, and spiritual energetic imbalances. Many energy healers and alternative health practitioners refer to this lack of ease in the body as "dis-ease." Crystal grids are an ideal solution to address the many causes of energetic imbalance. For example, a grid for autoimmune disease (see page 76) might address the energetic center, or chakra, that governs this type of illness and is most likely to be out of balance while also supporting the area of the body where that sickness manifests, such as the small intestine.

CREATIVITY

The human soul has many roles, and one of the most important is to create. Sometimes we create in obvious ways by drawing, dancing, or playing music, and other times we create without realizing it. Every day, for example, we create our own experiences through our thoughts, emotions, and actions, thereby building the world we inhabit, even if unintentionally.

When you begin to understand your role in the creation of your experience, you might find that your life starts to flow more effortlessly.

Understanding your creative potential causes you to think and act more intentionally. Crystal grids can help focus or amplify intention and boost the power of your creative processes. They can allow you to make more deliberate choices, whether through your daily activities and rituals or through creative expression.

PROSPERITY

It's human nature to want to lead a more prosperous life. The abundance of the universe is available to everyone who chooses to claim it. But prosperity can mean different things to different people. Some view it as wealth and financial well-being. Others believe prosperity is to possess all of the beautiful things that make life worth living—meaningful work, loving relationships, spirituality, vitality, good health, and more. One of the biggest blocks to experiencing prosperity is believing that there is not enough of what you most desire to go around. New Age and metaphysical experts call this concept a "consciousness of lack." Crystal grids can help remove this energy so you can become a magnet for all that you desire and value.

EMOTIONS

Emotions exist on an energetic spectrum of polar opposites. As humans, we desire the emotions we deem positive and struggle with the emotions we deem negative. It's important that we allow ourselves to feel whatever emotions arise in us, because when we suppress them, those feelings can get stuck and hinder our well-being. Creating crystal grids can help us positively process our emotions in three ways: First, they can inspire movement in the energy of our stuck emotions; second, they allow us to recognize all emotions as a valuable part of the human experience; and third, they guide us to move more quickly into the emotions we find desirable.

SPIRITUALITY

As embodied souls, our ultimate "work" when we are here is to remember who we truly are and eventually reunify with Source energy. This process is sometimes referred to as reaching enlightenment or Nirvana. Buddhists believe this can take multiple lifetimes to achieve. A state of enlightenment can develop over lifetimes as we begin to reclaim small pieces of our true selves through the human experience. Crystal grids can aid in this process, allowing you to connect to your true essence or receive Divine guidance by increasing intuition, helping to strip away layers of illusion, and more.

HOW GRIDS WORK

Crystal grids work via the synergy between the vibrations of multiple crystals and the energetic patterns they are arranged in, coupled with the intentions created by the use of sacred geometry. Each element refines and amplifies the others to create potent vibrational healing tools that are far more powerful than the sum of their parts.

A SIMPLE FORMULA FOR CRYSTAL GRIDS

How crystal grids work can be broken down into a simple formula:

Intention + Focus + Crystals + Shape = Outcome

A crystal grid requires each of the above elements in order to create the energetic environment necessary for a functional grid.

INTENTION

Intention is your lodestar, the guide that will get you from where you are to where you wish to be. It's usually a positive statement about how you want to feel rather than what you want. A general intention is often preferable to a very specific one (so you don't limit the range of things the universe can provide).

For example, a good, broad intention for abundance could be *I am joyful, generous, prosperous, and open to receive.* This intention allows the universe to work its magic without limitation. On the other hand, if your intention is *I make X dollars per year at my job*, you could limit the universe from sending you prosperity outside of your job or from providing you with even more than X dollars.

FOCUS

Creating a crystal grid is a way to mindfully focus on your intention and put it out into the universe. The more personal focus you dedicate to identifying your true intention and creating your grid, the more refined your intention and the stronger and more effective your grid will be. Seeing your grid each day will remind you to maintain focus on your intention and will enable the energy of the grid to magnetize your thoughts and pull your desired outcome to you.

CRYSTALS

Different crystals vibrate at their own unique frequencies (see chapter 2, page 13), and those frequencies support various intentions and outcomes. Within the structure of a grid, one crystal typically provides the overall intention while additional layers of crystals help expand, refine, and direct that intent. For example, in a grid for creative expression, the center stone would generate the intention of creativity, a second layer of stones might refine the intent for creativity through words or self-expression, and a third layer could draw creativity toward you or send it out into the world (or both).

SHAPE

Shapes have unique energy signatures, so arranging crystals into specific geometric patterns can strengthen or refine focus, support intention, and direct the energy in a broad or specific way.

INSPIRED BY NATURE AND DESIGN

Grid shapes appear over and over in nature and in human-facilitated design. The layouts of these grids, whether simple or complex, create inspired and beautiful designs based on sacred geometric shapes that contribute energetic power.

FIBONACCI SPIRALS AND THE GOLDEN RATIO

The Fibonacci sequence—named after famed Italian mathematician Leonardo Bonacci—appears in countless natural spirals, such as nautilus shells, pinecones, romanesco broccoli, and sunflowers. Numerically it looks like this: 0, 1, 1, 2, 3, 5, 8, 13, 21, 34, and so on. The sequence is based on adding the previous two numbers together to get the next number. The ratio between each pair of numbers (1.618034) is called the golden ratio, the golden mean, or phi. While found in nature, this ratio has also been used in architectural wonders, such as the Acropolis and the Great Mosque of Kairouan.

GREAT PYRAMID OF GIZA

The Great Pyramid of Giza in Egypt is built with dimensions that vary from phi by only 0.25 percent. It was built by hand during the reign of Khufu, which lasted from 2589 to 2566 BCE.

STONEHENGE

Built in stages between 3000 and 1500 BCE, this formation of monoliths in Wiltshire, England, takes the simple, sacred geometric shape of a circle. The monument is oriented to the rising sun on summer solstice, and although theories abound, its original purpose remains a mystery.

THE PARTHENON

Ancient Greece's Athenian temple, the Parthenon, was built between 447 and 432 BCE as part of the Acropolis complex to shelter a statue of the Goddess Athena. The golden ratio was applied throughout the design, including to the height and width of the marble columns. The foundation was also made of limestone, another energetic stone.

SACRED GEOMETRY

The repetition of certain shapes and patterns in both human-made structures and throughout nature suggests they are not random but are imbued with meaning. Replicating the proportions of these divinely inspired sacred geometries in crystal grids, art, and other objects allows us to bring the Divine into our daily lives.

Each sacred geometric shape has its own special meaning and vibrates with its own energy. In gridwork, you can return to these shapes and their variations again and again in order to bring more energy, focus, and meaning to your grids.

CIRCLE

Circles are the perfect representation of singularity and oneness. They also represent continuity and infinite flow. For example, the ancient symbol of the ouroboros depicts a snake in a perfect circle eating its own tail, which represents the universal concepts of infinity, oneness, and the cyclical nature of all things. Circles can also symbolize protection and regeneration. Likewise, the yin-yang symbol is circular, showing the endless cycle and balance of energetic opposites and how each side of the opposite is necessary for the existence of the whole. Sacred geometric forms made from circles include the following:

- Vesica piscis: 2 overlapping circles side by side
- Seed of life: 6 overlapping circles as well as a central circle
- Flower of life: 19 overlapping circles within a circle

SPIRAL

Spirals arise from the Fibonacci sequence and the golden ratio. They are found throughout nature, as in the centers of sunflowers, and even in our solar system and distant galaxies. The unfolding of the spiral represents the eternal growth and expansion along one's path. Spirals also represent universal wisdom, the harmonic relationship between elements, and higher consciousness. You'll find spirals in various shapes:

- The triskelion, which is three spirals joined together at a common point to form a triangular shape
- Natural elements, such as a nautilus shell or the center of a sunflower
- Circles, which are variations of spirals; you can add a spiral to the inside of any circle

TRIANGLE

Triangles represent trinities such as body, mind, and spirit or the various states of creation (thought, word, and action). They can represent creation and creativity and the summoning of a higher power. Triangles with different orientations and lines through them represent the classical elements of Earth, Water, Fire, Air, and Ether. In addition, they can represent union, harmony, and stability.

Triangles are also found throughout nature and design:

◆ Geographical formations, such as mountains

◆ Squares, trapezoids, or rectangles, which can be composed of two triangles

◆ Pentagrams, hexagrams, the Star of David, and the Tree of Life

INTENTION IS KEY

Every crystal grid begins with an intention, and every intention begins with a desire. So, before you create your grid, it's essential that you come up with an intention that will serve your greatest good. I recommend starting with a single and simple intention, working with no more than two at the same time. Setting too many intentions can scatter your energy and can detract from the final outcomes you seek, just as pursuing several tasks at once decreases your ability to focus on individual goals.

Your primary intention should always be to serve your highest good, as well as the greatest good of the universe. Ask yourself, "What is it that I want most in my life? Why do I want it? How will I feel if I achieve or have it?" The answers to these questions will help you arrive at an intention for your grid.

You can also ask the universe, "What will serve my greatest good today?" It will respond in the form of intuition, which can reveal your intention for your grid.

I tried this for the first time many years ago. I'd been tooling around, setting very specific intentions. I was receiving those things I intended, yet I still felt vaguely dissatisfied and restless. I soon realized that what I really wanted was to feel like I was serving the universe in the way I was intended to.

That day, I revised my intentions from specific to more general requests: "Please allow me to serve the universe in the best way I can." As I listened to my intuition, I created a grid based on instinct. Every few days, I felt compelled to restate that intention and create a new grid. Quite quickly, things I was holding on to that no longer served me fell by the wayside. New opportunities I'd never imagined or expected came in their place. Interestingly, this was the start of my career as a writer and metaphysical teacher, and I have never looked back.

Occasionally, I create a grid for a specific intention. However, for the most part, my intention remains to serve the greatest universal good I can, and the Divine continues to respond with inspiration for grids and outcomes that pull me forward in that direction.

You can do the same thing, or you can choose to create grids based on more specific intentions. Either way, focus on living your purpose in a meaningful way that brings joy into your life, and the crystal grids will abide.

CHAPTER 2

How Crystals Work

EACH CRYSTAL VIBRATES at its own unique frequency, which corresponds to various physical and energetic aspects of the universe. Each crystal contains distinct properties that contribute to its overall purpose and the energy it is capable of attracting. These properties include a crystal's internal structure, type and shape, and color. It's possible to select crystals that vibrate at frequencies that will magnetize broad or specific intentions and draw them toward you. By selecting the correct crystal, you can energize any intention.

COLLECTIVE ENERGY

Imagine a single violin playing a melody. The sound of the solo is rich, beautiful, and pleasing. Hearing only the melody played on a single instrument allows you to understand the piece intimately. Now add additional instruments: a piano to accompany the melody, and then a cello to add harmony, a viola to play a counter-melody, and a string bass to add direction and movement. As a quintet, the piece takes on richness, complexity, and power while still maintaining the focus of the original melody played by a single instrument.

A grid is like a small symphony of crystals. A single gemstone sets the tone of the grid and is powerful and beautiful by itself. Adding additional crystals weaves in harmonious, descriptive, and broadening elements and movement, while the grid's geometry provides an overall direction or structure. However, even with all of the other elements adding potency to the single initial gemstone, its "melody" remains in the form of your intention for the grid. Adding the geometry and additional crystals enhances the true purpose of the original crystal without detracting from the purity of its contribution.

When it comes to healing, crystals work via the Law of Attraction, which suggests that like energy attracts like energy, and entrainment, a principle of physics in which two objects vibrating at different frequencies "lock into phase" and begin to vibrate at the same frequency when they are near each other. Simply put, your thoughts, words, and actions determine the outcomes and elements you draw into your life. For example, if you think, speak, and act as if you are joyful, you are both more likely to attract joyful circumstances and feelings and more likely to choose joy as your main emotion. If you think, speak, and act angry, then you are both more likely to attract circumstances that make you feel angry and more likely to choose anger as your dominant emotion.

Crystals, both individually and within grids, support the Law of Attraction by providing a way to focus your intention through their vibrational frequency. They also serve as a reminder of your intention, which makes you more likely to engage in thoughts, words, and actions that attract what you desire. When you place crystals in a space you inhabit, they can entrain that area and everything in it (including you) to their frequency so you can intentionally attract certain elements and outcomes into your life.

The more crystals you use, the stronger this attraction will be, provided the crystals all support your intention. If you use crystals that are counterintuitive to your intention, you may send confusing messages out into the universe. In gridwork, the universe responds to conflicting intentions by either disregarding them or by providing the outcome related to your most dominant and frequent thought. That's why working with crystals that support your intentions is so important. Keeping things simple and focusing on just a few choice crystals and intentions at a time will help you avoid the trap of trying to use lots of different crystals to achieve everything you desire at once.

CRYSTAL LATTICE SYSTEMS

A crystal's vibration and purpose is dependent on its internal lattice—how the atoms are arranged within a crystal. These lattice systems are microscopic and undetectable to the naked eye, but they affect the vibrational frequency of the crystals and the type of energy they magnetize. Following are descriptions of the six basic crystalline lattices and lists of crystals that exemplify each lattice system. Note that the crystals I utilize in the grids in part 2 have been called out with asterisks.

MONOCLINIC

Monoclinic crystals protect and expand. They facilitate growth in all aspects of your being. The following common crystals contain a monoclinic lattice:

- Charoite
- Epidote
- Gypsum
- Kunzite
- Lepidolite*
- Malachite
- Moonstone*
- Selenite*
- Serpentine

TRICLINIC

Crystals with a triclinic lattice system can help balance and harmonize energies. They also repel or absorb energy that doesn't serve your highest good and allow you to contain and hold on to energy that does. Common crystals with a triclinic lattice system include the following:

- Amazonite
- Kyanite
- Labradorite* (rainbow moonstone)
- Sunstone
- Turquoise*

HEXAGONAL

Crystals with a hexagonal structure energize, magnetize, and attract. They can amplify existing energy and help you manifest things in your life. Hexagonal crystals are sometimes called rhombohedral. Many of the crystals used in the grids in this book have a hexagonal lattice structure:

- Agate*
- Amethyst*
- Ametrine*
- Apatite
- Aquamarine
- Aventurine
- Calcite*
- Carnelian*
- Chalcedony*
- Citrine*

- Clear quartz*
- Emerald
- Jasper
- Rose quartz*
- Smoky quartz*
- Tiger's-eye*
- Tourmaline*

ISOMETRIC

Isometric crystals are also sometimes called cubic. They can help improve energy associated with the physical, so they are good for focusing on health situations. Isometric crystals also provide stability and grounding. These are crystals with an isometric lattice system:

- Diamond
- Fluorite*
- Garnet*
- Pyrite*
- Sodalite*

ORTHORHOMBIC

Crystals with an orthorhombic (rectangular) lattice system cleanse and purify energy. They also clear and remove blocked energy and can help you get "unstuck." Common crystals with an orthorhombic lattice system include the following:

- Angelite
- Celestite*
- Chrysocolla
- Danburite
- Iolite (cordierite)
- Peridot*
- Tanzanite
- Topaz

The lattice structure of tetragonal crystals is similar to the orthorhombic lattice structure in that it is also rectangular, but the base of the internal rectangular formations is square. You can use tetragonal crystals to attract specific energies into your life; they work like magnets. They can amplify positive energy and block or absorb negative energy. I haven't included any tetragonal crystals in the grids in this book because there are plenty of other more affordable and readily available crystal options to choose from that have similar energetic traits. However, if you already have tetragonal crystals, please feel free to use them. These are most common:

- Apophyllite
- Rutile (often found in quartz)
- Zeolite
- Zircon

There are also certain materials used as healing crystals that don't have an internal lattice structure. Though I'll call them "crystals" in this book, know that geologically they aren't technically crystals. However, they still have various healing properties based on their color. These are the most commonly encountered stones in this class:

- Amber*
- Moldavite
- Obsidian (including snowflake obsidian)*
- Opal
- Pearl
- Petrified wood
- Tektite

EXTERNAL SHAPES

Crystals come in a wide variety of shapes and sizes. They can be cut into hearts, wands, spheres, or three-dimensional polyhedrons called Platonic solids (named after the philosopher Plato), and some varieties occur in natural clusters or points. Shape is important because it can affect how a crystal channels energy.

POINTS

Crystals, such as quartz and its variations, naturally occur in points. They differ from towers and pyramids in that these are natural formations and not carved or hand-shaped. Crystal points are usually oblong in shape with a point, or termination, on one end or both. Crystal points are good for gathering and directing energy. Position the termination in the direction you'd like to send its energy. You can use the flat end to gather energy, much like you would use a funnel. You can also turn a point to gather energy through the pointed end and widen or amplify it through the wide or flat end.

CLUSTERS

Clusters are another naturally occurring crystal shape, especially among some varieties of quartz. Clusters often work best at the center of grids. They diffuse energy and are ideal for sending energy throughout a larger space. You can even amplify and project a smaller crystal's energy by placing it in the center of a cluster of clear quartz.

PYRAMIDS

Some crystals naturally form a rough pyramid shape, but most are carved and shaped by hand. You can use pyramids much as you would use a crystal point—to gather and direct energy. They can also stabilize or anchor energy for a grid. For example, you might place four pyramids in each of the four corners of a grid to anchor the energy.

SPHERES

Spheres radiate energy all around them in an even pattern. Because of this, they often make excellent stones for the center of a grid. Spheres can also help strengthen intuition. They work especially well in grids that support creativity.

HEARTS

Crystals carved into heart shapes carry with them the vibration of love. This includes more than just romantic love—also unconditional love, Divine love, platonic love, familial love, and more. Anytime you need to feel more love in your life, a heart-shaped crystal can help attract and radiate this powerful emotion that is the driving energy behind everything in the universe. You can use heart-shaped crystals anywhere in a grid.

TOWERS/OBELISKS

Towers, or obelisks, are essentially crystals that are hand- or machine-carved into points. These differ from "points," which are naturally terminated crystal formations. They also differ from pyramids because they are elongated. Towers are oblong with a wide flat end and a narrower pointed end. They gather energy and direct it, and you can place them directionally in grids to send their energy out into space or toward a specific object or person. For example, for a sleep grid under your bed, you might place a few towers around the perimeter of the grid pointing upward to direct energy toward you as you sleep.

WANDS

Crystal wands may be faceted or smooth. Wands can be used to direct and focus energy in a specific direction or amplify the overall energy of a grid. They are particularly useful for directing energy for physical or chakra healing. One specific type of faceted crystal wand is called a Vogel crystal or a Vogel wand. It's carved in the shape of the Tree of Life from the Kabbalah, a shape representing the ten archetypal energies known as sefirot, which are the ten original words of creation, according to Kabbalistic beliefs. Vogel wands are very powerful energetic directors and amplifiers.

EGGS

Eggs are extremely strong and, because of their unique shape, have tremendous resistance to compression. A crystal carved into an egg shape is likewise imbued with strength. They are ideal for gathering strength and improving boundaries. Eggs are also a symbol of birth and new beginnings, so you can use egg-shaped crystals in grids that are focused on bringing something new into your life or bringing life to a new creation.

NATURAL VERSUS POLISHED

When you walk into a crystal shop, you'll discover uncarved, uncut stones in two different states: natural and tumbled/polished. Natural stones are unadulterated in any way. They tend to appear just as they did when they came out of the earth; they don't have a lot of external sheen, and they lack a specifically identifiable shape.

Tumbled and/or polished stones have been cut or polished by a person or a rock tumbler in order to emphasize color and inclusions. These stones are smooth and shiny.

Both natural and polished stones are equally effective in energy healing work; I've never noticed any difference between the two. Some people do feel there's a difference, so I suggest you rely on your intuition and see which feels best for you.

Whichever type of crystal shape speaks to you, remember that regardless of its state, it has gathered energy from anyone or anything that has come into contact with it. Therefore, it's essential that when you bring a new crystal home to work with in a grid, you cleanse it—which I will explain in chapter 4.

THE ROLE OF COLOR

The color of a crystal signifies its energetic properties. In fact, when we look at the color of any object, that color comes from energetic vibration at a specific frequency. This is why chakras are associated with colors that have similar vibrational frequencies. Crystals that correspond to a chakra's color also vibrate at the same frequency and can balance that chakra's energy.

BLACK/GRAY

Black and gray crystals are grounding and protective. They absorb negative energy or repel it altogether. Black crystals create energetic boundaries. They're often used around the perimeter of grids to keep out negative energy or to contain the energy of the grid within a certain space. Physically, black crystals can help with autoimmune conditions and addiction.

RED

Red crystals are grounding. Likewise, they're associated with passion. They can improve feelings of safety and security. Physically, both red and black crystals are associated with the root, or first, chakra and help with issues of the lower extremities, such as leg pain or gout, as well as certain mental health issues, such as depression and addiction.

BROWN

Brown crystals aid in issues of physical and emotional appetites by bringing balance. They also bring nurturing, support, and earth energy into situations. They are associated with the first and second chakras, so they can also be helpful regarding issues with the lower extremities and the lower abdominal region.

ORANGE

Orange crystals bring happiness and joy, and they support sexuality and a sense of self. Orange sparks creative inspiration, and it facilitates career growth and financial prosperity. Physically, orange is associated with your lower digestive system, as well as with your reproductive organs, lower back, and hips. It's also associated with the sacral, or second, chakra.

YELLOW/GOLD

Yellow and gold crystals improve self-esteem and confidence. Yellow supports the development of personal will. Physically, yellow is associated with the solar plexus, abdominal organs, and your adrenals, kidneys, liver, and pancreas. Yellow is also energizing. It balances the energy of the solar plexus, or third, chakra.

GREEN

Green crystals are linked to the heart, or fourth, chakra. Physically, this color supports issues of the heart, lungs, chest, rib cage, and middle back. Green also reduces anger and bitterness, increases feelings of love, and facilitates forgiveness.

PINK/ROSE

Pink and rose-colored crystals are associated with gentle and loving emotions, as well as with the heart chakra. Use these crystals to facilitate forgiveness, self-forgiveness, unconditional or romantic love, nurturing, kindness, compassion, and self-compassion. Physically, pink and rose crystals are associated with the heart, shoulders, arms, and hands. These are the best crystals to use in romantic situations.

BLUE/INDIGO

Blue crystals help with self-expression, creative expression, and speaking or living your truth. Blue crystals strengthen integrity, criticism, and judgment, and they allow you to give voice to the things that truly matter to you. These crystals help physically with issues of the throat, mouth, jaw, and ears and are associated with the throat, or fifth, chakra. Blue crystals can also create peace and lessen anxiety.

PURPLE/VIOLET

Purple or violet crystals are associated with the third eye, or sixth, chakra. They help improve memory, strengthen critical thinking skills, and improve sleep. Violet crystals can also strengthen intuition, help with intuitive dreams, and channel messages from your higher self and your spirit guides. Purple and violet are colors associated with psychic ability, so you can use them for intuitive development. Use purple and violet crystals to improve conditions associated with the eyes, nose, sinuses, and head. They are excellent for helping with migraines.

WHITE/CLEAR

White and clear crystals are associated with the top of your head and your crown, or seventh, chakra. Spiritually, they can connect you to Source energy. They can also amplify and strengthen the energy of other crystals. Physically, white or clear crystals can help improve issues of the muscular and skeletal systems and the skin. They can also help improve systemic issues, such as fibromyalgia.

CHAPTER 3

Grid Essentials

WORKING WITH GRIDS can be an intuitive or a formulaic process. I tend to employ a combination of both approaches. Use the information here as a starting point. When you feel ready, begin to explore and create your own crystal grids that have meaning for you.

ELEMENTS OF A GRID

At its most basic, a grid has a center stone for focus and a single perimeter of stones arranged into a simple geometric shape, such as a circle or a triangle. There's beauty and potency in simple grids that can energize and focus your intentions in a powerful way.

More complex grids incorporate a variety of crystals in a detailed layout with multiple layers. You can even add non-crystal elements, such as flowers, sea glass, shells, herbs, or other meaningful objects. This type of grid can also be powerful, provided you choose each element with intention. Most grids lie somewhere in between the simple and the complex. It's up to you to intuit what you feel will best suit your intention. As you decide, use the following elements for guidance.

FOCUS STONE

The focus of your crystal grid layout is the center stone. It anchors your main intention for the grid. Using our metaphor of a symphony from chapter 2, the focus stone is the grid's melody.

To find your focus stone, ask yourself, "What is my primary intention?" (See chapter 1, page 10, for tips on intention setting.) I also advise my students to determine the feeling they're trying to achieve with their intentions. For example, if your intention is prosperity, why do you want prosperity? What is it that you hope to feel or experience by being prosperous? This feeling is your grid's primary focus. Once this focus is established, you can choose the stone that will be most appropriate for your grid.

- Choose rose quartz for a grid focused on developing compassion.
- Choose citrine for a grid focused on self-esteem.
- Choose amethyst for a grid focused on spiritual connection.

DESIRE STONE

Desire stones typically form the layers immediately around the focus stone. Your grid may incorporate a single layer or involve several, depending on the type of grid and your preferences. The desire stone helps fine-tune, modify, or amplify the energy of your focus stone.

- A grid for a thyroid condition such as Hashimoto's disease could have a garnet focus stone to balance the first chakra, where autoimmune conditions originate. Since thyroid disease affects the throat, a smart choice for a desire stone would be chalcedony or celestite, to help energize that region of the body.
- A grid about creativity could have a focus stone of carnelian to boost creative ideas. A blue lace agate desire stone could bring creative ideas into expression. If you have plenty of creative ideas, but they never come to fruition, it may be due to an imbalance between the sacral chakra, where creative ideas are born, and the throat chakra, where creative expression occurs. These two colors stone can balance those chakras, creating a connection so you can express your creativity.
- For a grid to help you recall dreams, a good focus stone is amethyst, which supports the third eye chakra, where dreams and intuition arise. Black tourmaline, which supports the root chakra and provides grounding, would be a smart choice for a desire stone. This brings the content of dreams back into the body and anchors them in the physical so you can remember them.

DIRECTIONAL STONES

Directional stones—sometimes referred to as way stones—help direct the grid's energy where you want it to go. This is usually a single layer of stones forming the outer perimeter of the grid. Here are a few examples:

- Clear quartz points directed outward can push the energy of the grid out into a space.
- A perimeter of a triclinic stone such as turquoise can help contain the energy of the grid within the grid space.
- A perimeter of smoky quartz can transmute any negative energy to positive, giving the grid even more of a positive charge.
- A perimeter of selenite can cleanse the crystals in a grid, allowing them to retain their energetic structure for a longer period.

15 GRIDS TO GET
YOU STARTED

IN THIS SECTION, you'll find sample layouts for fifteen basic grids. For each, I'll explain the intention and meaning behind the shape, some sample grid uses, and suggestions about how to place the stones. You don't need to follow these instructions exactly like a recipe; rather, you can start with the basic shape and then choose your own crystals, elements, and placements. The grids are arranged based on geometric form, from the simplest version of that form (such as a single circle) to the most complex (such as a flower of life). Some grids will include optional layout ideas that you can use to create more complex or specific grids.

CIRCLE

The circle is the simplest form a grid can take. It's a great way to create a functional grid with a minimum number of stones. Circular grids send their energy outward into the universe in an even pattern and are often focused on integration and wholeness, such as the overall health of body, mind, and spirit. Historically, you'll find circles in art (as in the symbol of the ouroboros), architecture (as in domed structures), and various forms of spirituality (as in the yin-yang symbol in Taoism). Use five or more stones to make a circle grid.

MEANING

- Harmony
- Oneness
- Source
- Divine
- Eternal cycles, such as birth, life, death, and rebirth

LAYOUT BASICS

- Place the focus stone in the exact center of the circle.
- Place a perimeter of at least four stones (one at the apex of each arc). These can be either desire stones or directional stones.
- Optional: Add more layers around the original circle of additional desire stones or directional stones.

BEST USED TO

- Ground your energy
- Circulate energy
- Create physical healing
- Integrate body, mind, and spirit
- Connect to a higher power
- Reflect on the cycles of life
- Magnetize your intention to attract what you desire

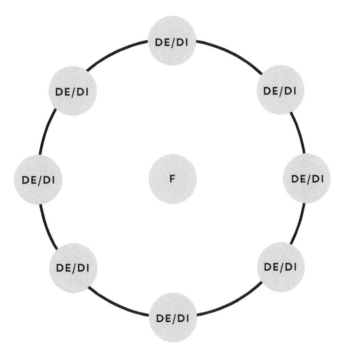

SUNBURST

The sunburst represents a halo of light around the basic shape of a circle. Using it as a decorative motif became popular during the Baroque period. You will need at least five stones to create a sunburst.

MEANING

◆ Fire and passion
◆ Purification
◆ Directional movement of energy outward

LAYOUT BASICS

◆ Make the focus stone the center of the sunburst.
◆ Place four or more crystal points with the flat ends facing the focus stone and the terminated (pointed) ends pointing out toward the room. These are directional stones.

◆ Optional: Make a multilayer sunburst by placing your focus stone in the center, then adding as many layers of desire stones as you wish in concentric circles around the focus stone. Finally, use crystal points as directional stones around the outer perimeter of the grid.

BEST USED TO

◆ Create warmth
◆ Boost your body's metabolic processes
◆ Improve mental, emotional, or spiritual clarity
◆ Increase or ignite creativity
◆ Ignite passion
◆ Strengthen willpower
◆ Energize your career
◆ Create positive energy and emotions, such as joy or enthusiasm

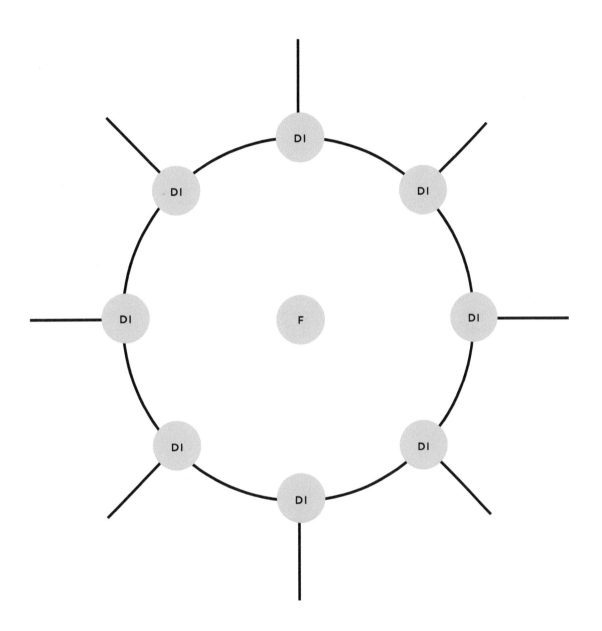

YIN-YANG SYMBOL

The yin-yang symbol has its roots in ancient China, with the earliest symbols found on oracle bones dating back to the fourteenth century BCE. The concepts of yin and yang are incorporated into various forms of Chinese philosophy, including Taoism, feng shui, and martial arts. A yin-yang grid is a variation on a circle grid—instead of one focus stone, the yin-yang grid has two. You will need at least six crystals to create a yin-yang grid, including two focus stones.

MEANING

Yin and yang represent important Taoist concepts:

- Balance
- Harmony
- Integration among two seemingly opposite energies
- Duality
- Apparent opposites coexisting on a spectrum and flowing into each other

LAYOUT BASICS

- Place the two focus stones as shown in the reference image. The focus stones should represent two elements in your life that you wish to bring into balance.
- Place at least four desire or directional stones around the focus stones in a circle.
- Optional: Create a grid with more than two layers. The inner layers will be desire stones, and the outer layers will be directional stones. Each layer will require at least four stones, but you can add more.

BEST USED TO

- Balance opposite energies in your life
- Ground Divine energy in earthly energy
- Integrate your conscious with your subconscious
- Balance and integrate body, mind, and spirit
- Recognize the illusory nature of life on the earthly plane

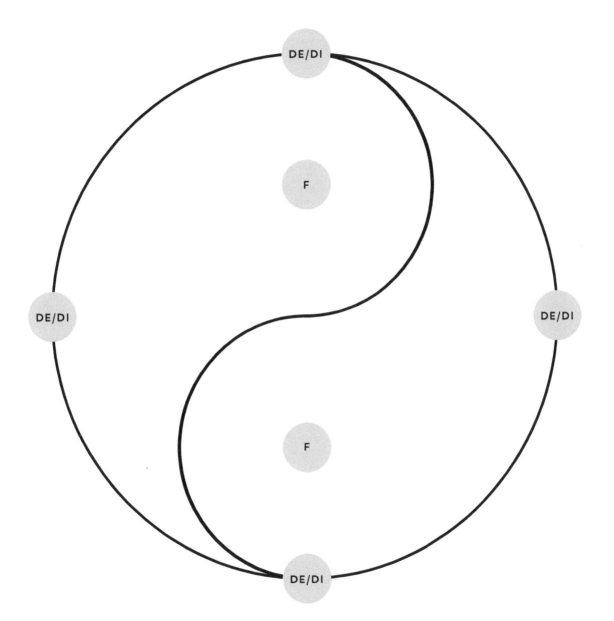

SPIRAL

Spirals begin at a center point and radiate outward following a mathematical formula and can continue outward infinitely. Two common types of spirals taught in geometry are the Archimedean spiral and the Fibonacci spiral (page 8). The Archimedean spiral moves outward uniformly along the straight line of a plane. Fortunately, you don't need to be that precise when creating a spiral grid; any type of spiral will do. Use as few as seven crystals or as many as you wish.

MEANING

- Unfolding of energy
- Personal growth
- Spiritual growth
- Movement of energy outward
- Journey along an unfolding path

LAYOUT BASICS

- Place your focus stone to begin the spiral.
- Working outward from the focus stone, place a combination of directional stones and desire stones.
- Intersperse directional stones with the desire stones by using point-shaped crystals to draw the energy ever outward in the spiral. I do this by alternating points (pointing in the direction of the unfolding spiral) with desire stones, but you can do it any way you wish.

BEST USED TO

- Create directed energy that moves constantly outward
- Spark spiritual awakening
- Outline your path as a soul
- Draw energy upward through your chakras
- Ground Divine energy by moving it downward through your chakras
- Spark growing and unfolding creativity
- Outline direction for your career path
- Move a project in a certain direction
- Awaken kundalini energy

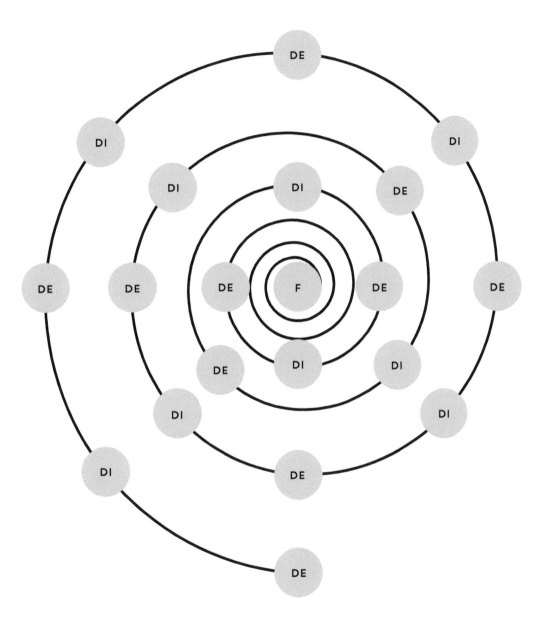

VESICA PISCIS

The vesica piscis is a sacred geometric shape that is composed of two overlapping circles. It's a Latin word that literally translates to "fish's bladder." It is most commonly recognized as a Christian symbol. In pre-Christian art, it is believed the vesica piscis was associated with female genitalia, sexuality, creation, and fertility. You will need eleven crystals to create a vesica piscis grid.

MEANING

- Divinity
- Balance
- Creation
- Infinity
- Union

LAYOUT BASICS

- Place the focus stone in the center of where the circles intersect.
- Place desire stones around the outside of the focus stone along the arcs of the two circles where they intersect.
- Place perimeter stones along the outside of the two circles where they don't intersect. These can be more desire stones, directional stones, or a combination of the two.

BEST USED TO

- Bring balance into various aspects of your life
- Connect to the Divine
- Integrate body, mind, and spirit
- Spur creativity
- Send intention or energy out into the infinite universe
- Create balance in imbalanced relationships
- Facilitate forgiveness
- Address sexual issues
- Improve fertility
- Bring together two sides of an issue to create consensus or compromise

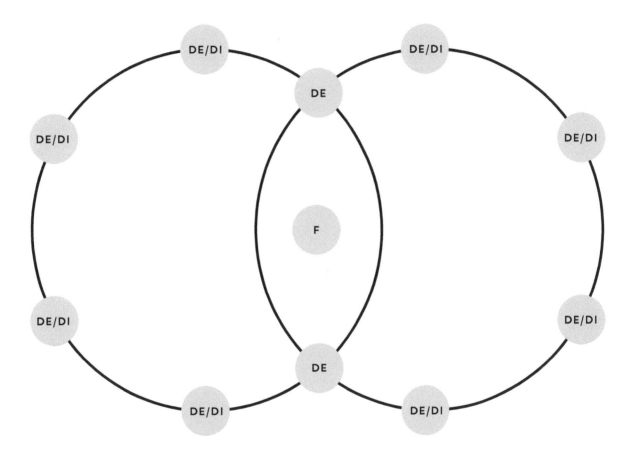

TRIQUETRA

The origin of the triquetra remains somewhat mysterious. Early depictions are found in both Celtic and Nordic art and artifacts from around 500 BCE. It is also commonly found in Celtic knot work from around the seventh century CE. In this iteration it's known as the Irish Trinity Knot. It is can also be formed in the center of another sacred Celtic geometric shape, the Celtic knot, which is the overlapping of three circles. You'll need at least seven stones for a triquetra.

MEANING

- Loyalty
- Love
- Friendship
- Faith
- Trinities (i.e., body, mind, and spirit)
- Protection

LAYOUT BASICS

- Place the focus stone in the very center where all three circles intersect.
- Place three desire stones around the center stone where the arcs of the three circles intersect.
- Put directional stones or additional desire stones at the points of the triquetra. You can also place directional stones in a circle around the triquetra.

BEST USED TO

- Protect against negativity
- Integrate body, mind, spirit
- Understand the greater nature of reality
- Help with anxiety and stress
- Help with depression
- Break free of destructive patterns
- Get out of a rut
- Attract wealth
- Improve conditions associated with ill health or dis-ease

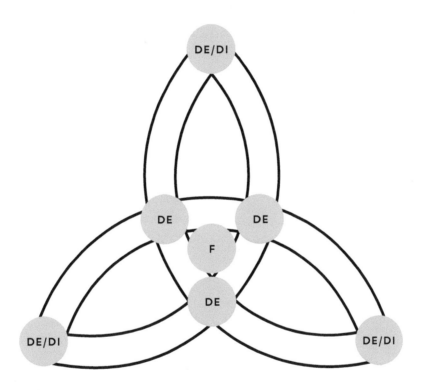

The seed of life is made of six overlapping circles arranged in a pattern, creating a six-petaled flower with a center point. Sometimes a seventh circle is drawn around the outside. The seed of life requires nineteen crystals.

By expanding the seed of life outward in six directions, you create a nineteen-circled image known as the flower of life. These two grids are a natural expansion from the circle and vesica piscis.

MEANING

- Divine guidance
- Source energy
- Expansion
- Creativity
- Spiritual growth

LAYOUT BASICS

- The following instructions, except the final one, guide you to create the seed of life. Expand it into the flower of life, if you desire.
- Place the focus stone in the very center of all of the circles where they intersect.
- Add a layer of desire stones at the point of each petal of the flower created by the intersection of circles.
- Add another layer of either desire stones, directional stones, or a combination at the point of the six larger petals at the intersection of the outer arcs of the circles.
- Optional: Add another layer of desire or directional stones at the apex of the arcs of each circle, and another layer around the arc of the outer circle of directional stones.
- Optional: For the flower of life, use a similar pattern with one focus stone in the very center. Then add desire stones at all of the center points of each flower and focus stones at the outer points of each petal along the outer rim of the flower.

BEST USED TO

- Germinate new ideas
- Address fertility, reproductive, and pregnancy issues
- Create positive energy
- Connect to Divine guidance
- Connect to Source energy
- Deepen meditation
- Expand your relationships, career, or any other energy you'd like more of in your life

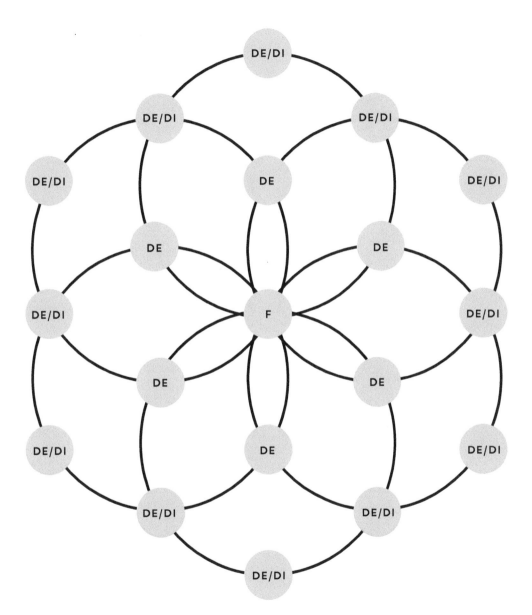

LOTUS

In Buddhism, the lotus represents the unfolding of purity of thought and deed from imperfection; just as the lotus blooms beautifully from mud, so can spirituality unfold from an imperfect human base. The flower is created from different orientations of the central section of a vesica piscis (page 38). You'll need thirteen stones to create a lotus grid.

MEANING

- Eloquent communication
- Spiritual unfolding

LAYOUT BASICS

- The lotus flower grid has one central petal and six surrounding oblong petals.
- Place the focus stone in the center of the central petal.
- Place desire stones at the arc apex of the central petal, the points of each petal, the intersection of the petals, and the outer arc of the outer petals.
- Optional: Add directional stones in a circle around the outside of the lotus.

BEST USED TO

- Deepen meditation or create meditative spaces
- Increase the power of affirmation and visualization
- Foster or spark spiritual growth
- Facilitate communication and connection with the Divine or Source energy
- Enhance spiritual learning
- Work with karmic issues

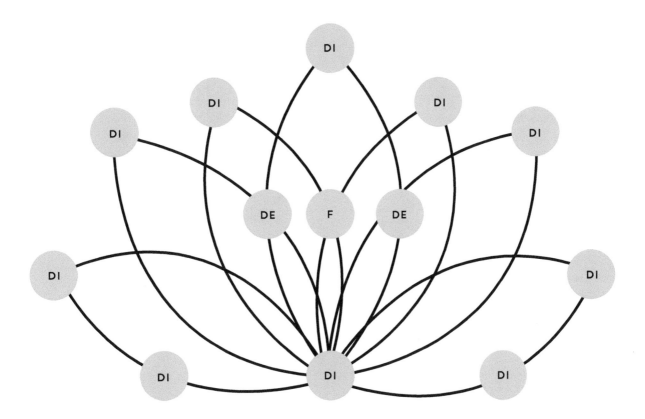

TRIANGLE

The triangle is a simple but powerful grid you can use alone or to serve as the basis of more complex grids. Triangles are a basic polygon consisting of three lines and three angles. In gridwork, you'll often use an equilateral triangle which has three sides that are roughly equal in length and internal angles that add up to 180 degrees. A basic triangle grid requires only four crystals (center and three points), but you can use more if you wish.

MEANING

The orientation and placement of the focus stone may affect the meaning of the grid.

◆ Stability
◆ Creation
◆ Classical elements of Water, Earth, Wind, Air, Ether, and Fire (depends on orientation—see illustration)

LAYOUT BASICS

◆ Place the focus stone at the center of the triangle.
◆ Place the desire stones at the apex of each angle.
◆ Optional: The chart shows the triangle orientation for each of the five classical elements. Each of these orientations can utilize the basic grid layout. For Ether, make the center stone the point where the two triangles meet. For Air and Earth, add one crystal on either side of the center stone along the sides of the triangle.
◆ Optional: Enclose the triangle in a circle, creating a perimeter of directional stones.

BEST USED TO

◆ Balance elemental energies of Earth, Air, Fire, Water, and Ether
◆ Strengthen any of the elemental energies
◆ Complement other energy healing modalities to bring balance and harmony
◆ Spark creativity
◆ Bring balance to triads such as body, mind, and spirit
◆ Recognize the true essence of reality

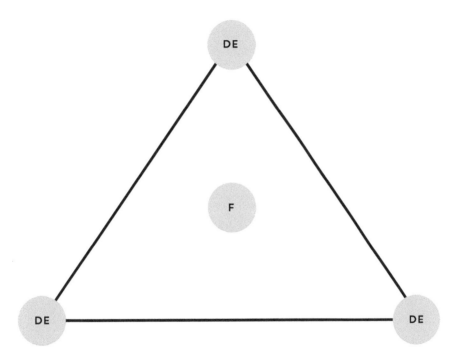

WATER

FIRE

AIR

ETHER

EARTH

TRISKELION

The triskelion (or triskele) is known as the spiral of life. Whatever you choose to call it, the symbol is created with three spirals originating from a common center point that collectively form a pyramid shape. The triskelion has appeared in the art of many cultures throughout the world since at least 4000 BCE. It even appears on the seal of the United States Department of Transportation. You'll need at least thirteen stones to create a triskelion.

MEANING

- Similar to the meaning of a spiral (page 9)
- Movement and growth on all three planes of human existence: body, mind, and spirit
- Outward movement from a source
- Cycles, such as past, present, and future or birth, life, and death

LAYOUT BASICS

- Place the focus stone at the center of the triskelion so it is the source point for each of the three spirals.
- Use four stones for each spiral.
- Place the desire stone at the center of each spiral.
- Place the remaining stones at the peak of each arch. These can be directional stones, desire stones, or a combination of both.
- Optional: Enclose the triskelion in a circle of stones.

BEST USED TO

- Work with karmic issues
- Deal with grief after the death of a loved one
- Integrate the paths of body, mind, and spirit
- Come to terms with the past and displace worry about the future
- Live in the present and focus on the eternal moment of now

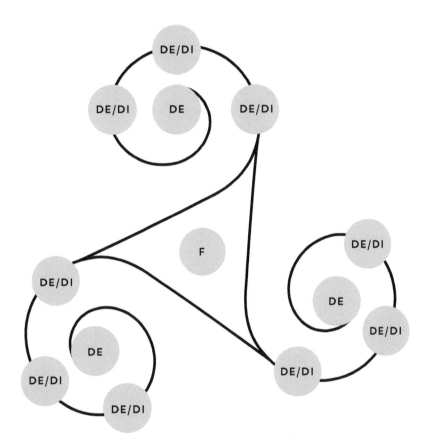

PENTAGRAM

Depictions of pentagrams have been found from as early as 6000 BCE, and the symbol has been used by many cultures, including Sumerian and Greek. During the Middle Ages in Europe, it became associated with occultism. A pentagram may be encased in a pentagon, or it might be a star within a circle. You need eleven stones for a pentagram grid.

MEANING

- The heavens
- Heaven and earth
- Magic
- Manifestation
- Truth
- Perfection
- Protection
- Earth
- Nature
- The classical elements

LAYOUT BASICS

- Place the focus stone in the very center of the star.
- Place desire crystals where the lines that make the pentagram intersect.
- Place desire or directional crystals at the points of each starburst.
- Optional: Add a perimeter layer of directional stones by creating a circle around the star.

BEST USED TO

- Connect to nature
- Ground yourself
- Manifest things you desire
- Bring together disparate elements to create something more powerful than the sum of its parts
- Honor the solstices, equinoxes, and other pagan seasonal celebrations
- Live and speak your truth
- Reduce criticism and judgment
- Protect against negativity

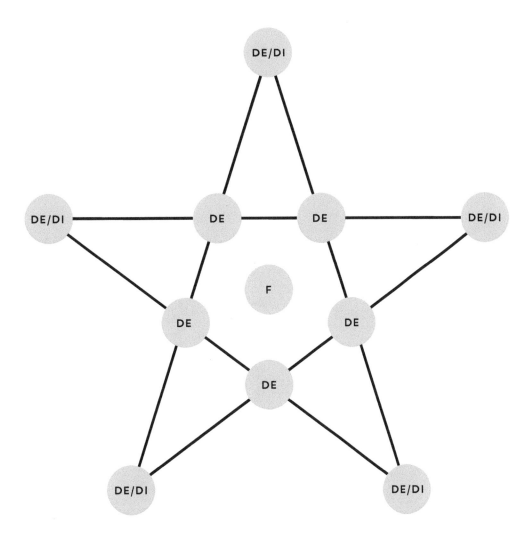

STAR OF DAVID

The Star of David is most commonly recognized as a Hebrew symbol. The six-pointed star is formed by combining two equilateral triangles, one pointing up, and one pointing down. Its shape is said to be based on the protective shield of King David. In Kabbalah, this symbol connects the kingdom of God to the kingdom of Man. You will need thirteen stones to make a Star of David grid.

MEANING

- Protection
- Seven spiritual building blocks: kindness, severity, harmony, perseverance, splendor, foundation, and royalty (six points of the star plus the center point)
- Joining of two halves of a whole
- Unity

LAYOUT BASICS

- Place the focus stone in the very center of the star.
- Place desire stones around the hexagon that is made by the intersection of the triangles on the inside of the star.
- Place directional stones at the peak of each triangle forming the points of the star.
- Optional: To simplify, remove the inner stones that make the hexagon. Place directional stones, desire stones, or a combination at the outer peaks of the triangles. In this case, you will only need seven crystals to make a Star of David.

BEST USED TO

- Protect against negative energy or thinking
- Undo negative thought patterns
- Grow spiritually
- Create unity
- Generate peace
- Attract a partner
- Balance and harmonize opposite energies

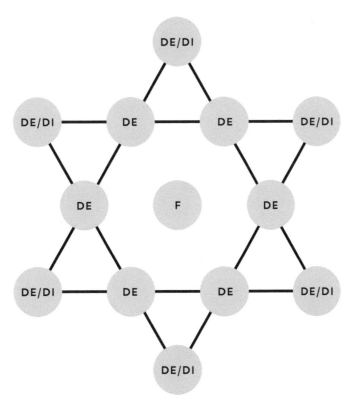

TREE OF LIFE

The Tree of Life is a Kabbalistic symbol that can also be found within the sacred geometric symbol of the Flower of Life (page 42). The Tree of Life represents the archetypal energies present in the life of man. It's believed that the symbol first appeared around the ninth century BCE in Assyria. You need ten crystals to create a Tree of Life grid.

MEANING

- Path to God
- Provides a blueprint for universal truth and ultimate reality
- Represents the ten energy centers, or sefirot, found in Kabbalah. These include:
  - Divine crown (1)
  - Wisdom (2)
  - Understanding (3)
  - Mercy (4)
  - Justice or strength (5)
  - Beauty (6)
  - Victory (7)
  - Splendor (8)
  - Foundation (9)
  - The power of physical healing (10)

LAYOUT BASICS

- Place the focus stone at the center of the tree (6). In the image, it's the top center stone.
- Place a secondary focus stone in spot 9.
- Place the remaining stones as desire stones.
- Optional: Use one crystal to represent each of the ten sefirot.

BEST USED TO

- Facilitate the integration of body, mind, and spirit
- Balance the body's energy centers (chakras)
- Create a path to the Source
- Connect with a higher power
- Strengthen faith

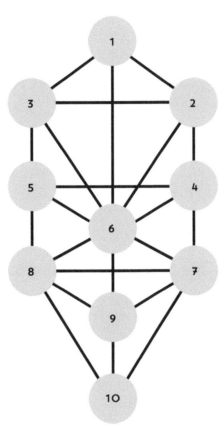

TIBETAN KNOT

Also known as the "endless knot" or "eternal knot," this knot design is one of Tibetan Buddhism's Eight Auspicious Symbols. Its first known appearance is on clay tablets from the Indus Valley Civilization in about 2500 BCE. You need fifteen crystals to create a Tibetan knot grid.

MEANING

- Connection between all aspects of being
- Connection between everything in the universe
- Eternal cycles such as birth, death, and rebirth
- Represents the "Zero Point Field," or the quantum interconnection of the universe that underlies reality

LAYOUT BASICS

- Place the focus crystal at the very center of the grid where the lines of the knot intersect.
- Place desire and/or directional crystals on the outer points of each of the knots.
- Optional: To make the grid more complex, place desire crystals wherever lines intersect on the grid, or in the open spaces between the intersections of the lines. Then place the directional crystals around the external points of the knot.

BEST USED TO

- Connect with spiritual principles
- Deepen or facilitate meditation
- Uncover the true nature of reality
- Join together seemingly disparate energies
- Help alleviate grief after the death of a loved one
- Strengthen connection to others in your life

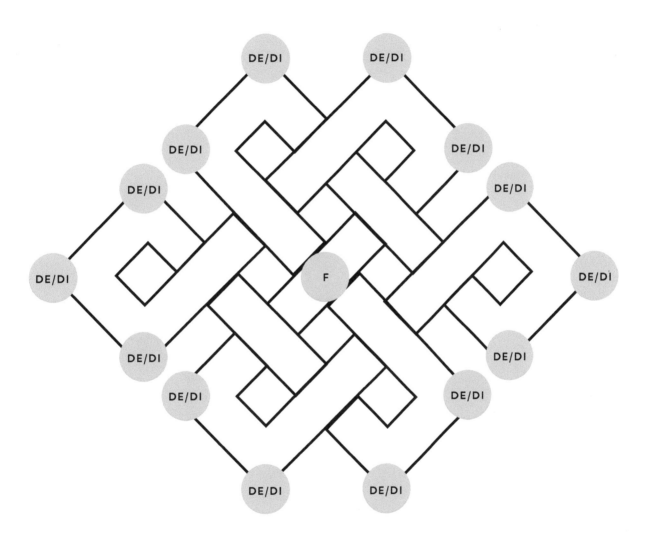

OM

Om (Aum) is not a geometric shape, but rather an ancient Sanskrit character that represents the sound of the universe. It first appeared in the Vedas at around 1500 BCE. It is commonly used as a meditative mantra and in practices such as yoga and chanting. You can use as many or as few stones as you'd like for an Om grid, although typically it takes around thirteen.

MEANING

Om is a way of summoning the power of the universe and uniting with it. It is a mantra, a prayer, an invocation, and a meditation.

- Mantra
- Universal truth
- God
- Source energy
- Higher insight
- Peace
- Understanding
- Compassion
- Enlightenment

LAYOUT BASICS

- Use the Om character as a guideline shape to lay out your crystals whenever you wish to invoke the idea of whatever Om means to you.
- There are no "rules" when it comes to laying out an Om grid.
- There is no focus stone (unless you want there to be one).
- There are no desire stones or directional stones.

BEST USED TO

- Invoke the power of the universe or unite with oneness and Source via meditation or prayer
- Release anxiety and invoke peace
- Engender kindness and compassion
- Strengthen wisdom
- Seek enlightenment
- Allow the universe to be in the driver's seat
- Walk your eternal path
- Focus on the now

CHAPTER 4

Working with Grids

NOW THAT YOU UNDERSTAND the basics of crystals and grid shapes, you're ready to begin creating on your own. In this chapter, we'll discuss the things you need to consider and do to ensure your grid works in the way you intend. To help you better understand the process, we'll focus on a specific example intention: finding a romantic relationship.

SET YOUR INTENTION

Intention drives all energy healing work. Your intention determines the materials you use and the shapes you create, as well as where to place your grid and how to interact with it.

Your intention is a statement of choice. It can be a specific idea, such as, "I will enter a romantic relationship with Steven." But as I stated in chapter 1, I caution you to avoid such a direct ask of the universe. Naming a very detailed and specific intention can cause you to miss out on something that serves your greatest good. It's better to focus on the feeling behind the intention. Instead of a romantic relationship with Steven, consider a broader intention, such as, "I am engaged in a dynamic and meaningful romantic relationship that serves my greatest good."

This leaves the universe a lot of room to provide you with the thriving relationship you desire, instead of limiting its choices to a single person who may or may not be the right partner for you.

To create an intention:

◆ Focus on the feeling or state of being you are trying to achieve instead of specific details.

◆ Create the intention as a statement of positivity, as if you have already received it. What you desire is already on the way to you, and the universe is just waiting for you to choose it so it can be delivered.

◆ Your intention can be written, spoken, thought, or visualized.

◆ If it's a written intention, fold the paper it's written on and place it under the focus stone of your grid.

◆ Only work on one or two intentions at a time.

CHOOSE YOUR GRID

With your intention firmly in mind, take a look at the grid shapes in the previous chapter and choose the one that best suits your purpose. If this is your first venture into gridwork, I encourage you to use the resources in this book. Once you get the hang of it, you may feel guided to create a different shape. For your first grid, choose a simple shape with two or three layers.

- Look through the grid shapes with your intention in mind and choose the one that jumps out at you.
- Read through each grid shape description to find the one that has the properties you feel best fit with your intention.
- For the intention to attract a romantic relationship, the Star of David or vesica piscis would be a good grid shape to start with.

CHOOSE YOUR CRYSTALS

Now that you have an understanding of crystals' different shapes, colors, and internal lattice structures, it's time to select which crystals to use for your grid. If you need additional support, see the list on page 174 for a quick reference. Here is an example for a relationship grid, which is one of the most common intention questions I get when teaching gridwork.

- To help support romantic and unconditional love, a rose quartz as your focus stone is a great place to start.
- Joy is usually the intended outcome of a romantic partnership, so choose stones that facilitate this emotion, such as amber or carnelian, as your layer (or layers) of desire stones.
- How do you want your intention to manifest in your life? Through the powerful experience of love. To amplify and direct those feelings into your life, clear quartz points are a good choice for the exterior perimeter of your grid.

TRUST YOUR INTUITION

I give you a lot of suggestions and recommendations in this book, but I also want you to know that there are no right or wrong choices in gridwork. What truly matters is the intention and the meaning behind it. In my classes, I always encourage students to work intuitively. Doing so causes your grid to take on deeper layers of meaning, because you've listened to your higher guidance system to create something that uniquely supports your intention.

To work intuitively:

1. Close your eyes and focus on your intention. Really take time to allow yourself to feel the fulfillment of your intention.

2. Once you truly feel deeply connected to your intention and the emotions behind it, ask, "What shape of grid will serve best here?" Let a specific shape or image come to mind. If nothing appears, scan through possible grid shapes and see what jumps out at you.

3. Now ask, "Which crystal best serves as a focus stone?" Pick up stones and hold them in your nondominant hand, your receiving hand. When one feels right, use it as your focus stone.

4. Do the same for directional and desire stones.

QUICK BUYING GUIDE FOR CRYSTALS

Although there is usually an exchange of money when you partner with crystals, I prefer to use the term "adopting" crystals rather than "buying." "Adopting" implies partnership or stewardship versus ownership. Before entering the shop, pause and clear your mind; ask for guidance in choosing the crystals that will work best with and for you. Once you enter a shop, pause and notice if you're pulled in any direction and follow that pull.

♦ When you see a crystal that sparks your interest, put it in your nondominant hand. Close your eyes and notice how it feels. Is there a "click" or connection? It could be a pleasant physical sensation, or a sense of peace or calm. Listen to this intuition. Base your choice first on how the crystal makes you feel, then on its shape.

♦ Don't feel pressured to spend a fortune on your crystals. Inexpensive crystals are equally as powerful as more high-end crystals, especially for gridwork. The basic crystals listed on page 174 are affordable, widely available, and can accomplish virtually anything.

♦ Size doesn't really matter, either, unless you're purchasing crystals for display. Smaller crystals work well for gridwork because you often need to use several of the same stone, plus they're more widely available and affordable.

♦ To keep costs down, consider buying affordable crystals in bulk on auction sites such as eBay. As long as you cleanse them upon arrival, they'll serve your grid well.

PREP WITH CARE

Cleansing and recharging crystals is an important aspect of energy hygiene. I mentioned the principle of entrainment in chapter 2, noting that when two objects of different vibrations are near each other, they can lock into phase. This phenomenon usually lowers the vibration of a crystal and raises the vibration of the nearby object. Cleansing and recharging helps return the crystals to their original high vibration.

CLEANSING

Cleanse your crystals before using them the first time and after they've worked especially hard. Be sure to hold them over the smoke of either sage or palo santo for about ten seconds or so. Another option is to place them out in moonlight or sunlight for one night or one day.

- Cleanse all crystals at least once a week.
- If you're going through a difficult or extremely emotional time, cleanse them daily.
- During periods of negativity or in a particularly intense grid, cleanse them every few days.
- Always cleanse crystals before you place them in a new grid.

CHARGING

Charging crystals involves programming them with specific intentions. It's good practice to charge your focus stone and desire stones before placing them in the grid. To charge crystals:

- Hold the crystals in your dominant hand, which is your giving hand.
- Close your eyes and visualize your intention, or repeat it as an affirmation aloud or in your mind.
- Feel the fulfillment of your intention; allow the positive emotions to flow through you and radiate all around you from your heart center.
- Be in tune with those positive emotions that flow from your heart to your arm and hand and into the crystal. Hold the crystal for as long as the positive emotions remain or until you feel guided to stop. Your crystals are now charged with your intention.

SEEK A LOCATION

There are several different ways to decide where to place your grid. You can place grids intuitively, according to principles of feng shui, or in places where their purpose makes sense (such as placing a grid for romance in your bedroom).

INTUITION

Close your eyes, and with your intention in mind, ask, "Where will it best serve to place this grid?" Then, go where you're drawn. Intuition is my favorite approach in selecting grid placement.

FENG SHUI

Feng shui is the Chinese art of placement. It suggests that various areas of your home support different types of energy. Traditionally, it relies on a compass and land formations. The map pictured here is known as the Black Hat Feng Shui, a Westernized version of feng shui. According to feng shui principles, everything is positioned in relation to the wall where the front door is located.

To use this map, stand inside your home at your front door with your back to the front door. Hold the map in front of you with the Career and Soul Path square at the bottom and Reputation and Fame at the top. Then, use the map to place grids in the areas of your home, work, or other spaces. For example, if your grid is for prosperity, place it in the back left corner of your home, office, or room, from the entrance facing in.

PURPOSE

You can also place grids in specific areas of your home that serve the purpose associated with your intention. For example, a grid to improve sleep will likely be most useful in your bedroom under your bed. A grid to help with willpower associated with food is probably best placed in your kitchen. A grid to help with career development might be best in your office.

BLACK HAT FENG SHUI

PROSPERITY & WEALTH	REPUTATION & FAME	RELATIONSHIPS & LOVE
HEALTH & FAMILY	SELF	CREATIVITY & CHILDREN
WISDOM & KNOWLEDGE	CAREER & SOUL PATH	TRAVEL & MENTORS

HOW LONG SHOULD YOUR GRID STAY INTACT?

I like to compare crystal gridwork to mandala sand paintings created by Tibetan Buddhist monks. While the monks create intricate and colorful works of art from carefully laid sand, their focus is meditative, but the nature of their art is temporary. After consecrating the finished art, the monks ritually sweep away the sand, because the mandalas are never meant to be permanent. The purpose was meditation, focus, and to recognize the temporary nature of all experience on Earth.

Likewise, your grid isn't meant to be permanent. You may make a grid, meditate and focus on it, and immediately remove it. You might keep it up for a week. Beyond seven days, I recommend reevaluating your intention, removing your grid, and creating a new one. In this way, you can ebb and flow with the energy of your own spiritual path.

When the monks sweep away their sand paintings, they do so with the intention of sending the energy into the universe and returning the sand to the Earth. I, too, recommend removing each stone mindfully as you offer gratitude for the work it has done for and with you.

PLACE AND ACTIVATE

The principles in this book can serve as guidelines, but if you have a sudden inspiration to try something different, go with that, as your intuition exists to guide you.

Start your grid by being in a meditative space. Sit quietly, place your hands over your heart, close your eyes, and focus on your heart center. Think of something that brings you joy—your children, a pet, a piece of music—whatever works for you.

- When you're in this positive state, visualize your intention. Speak it as an affirmation or write it down on a piece of paper. Breathe deeply as you do this, remaining in a relaxed and peaceful state.
- Hold your focus stone in your dominant hand and charge it with your intention.
- If you've written your intention as an affirmation, fold it and place it under the focus stone.

- Place your focus stone on the grid.
- Hold your desire stones in both hands and charge them with your intention. Place them in the grid. Do this for as many layers as you need, working with one set of stones at a time.
- Finally, place your directional stones.

What you do next is up to you. I encourage you to sit and look at your grid, visualizing your intention in your mind's eye; silently or verbally restate your intention as an affirmation. Before you walk away and go on about your day, give thanks to the universe, the grid, the source of your inspiration, your higher self, and the crystals within the grid. Take comfort in knowing that they are working to create the life you choose.

PART 2

CRYSTAL GRIDWORK IN ACTION

CHAPTER 5

Support Your Health and Wellness

IN OUR WESTERN SOCIETY, we tend to associate health and wellness with an absence of symptoms. Usually we only seek treatment when we experience negative symptoms. In reality, our health and wellness require much more attention. Symptoms are the body's alarm system which, if ignored, can sometimes turn into a severe illness.

Years ago, I had a number of mild symptoms that were warning signs of celiac disease: mild stomach pain, slight headaches, tiredness, and a little acid reflux. As the symptoms progressed, I treated it with Tums and my headaches with Excedrin. I slept a little more or consumed more caffeine.

This worked for a while, but eventually the medication was no longer effective. My symptoms grew so severe that I became malnourished. If I wanted to feel better, I needed to uncover and address the root of the problem. I had an intolerance to gluten, and had to stop eating it.

But until I took care of the root cause (gluten) of my symptoms (headaches, stomach pain, bruising, etc.), I wasn't going to get rid of my symptoms permanently.

The grids in this chapter are designed to address your body, mind, and spirit in order to prevent and heal what I call "dis-ease." Some of the grids focus on physical symptoms, while others focus on emotional, spiritual, and energetic issues. The goal of each grid is to create balance so that your body can return to its desired state of wellness. Note: It is important to see your doctor if you think you may have an illness.

IMMUNE SYSTEM STRENGTHENING

Shape: Circle
Type: Balancing and Strengthening

In our modern society, we live in a near-constant state of stress. Day-to-day living can weaken the immune system. This constant release of hormones from our adrenal glands negatively affects our sleep and metabolism, and even our immune systems. This grid is designed to strengthen the immune system so you can more effectively fight off illness and dis-ease.

FOCUS STONE—GREEN CALCITE

Since daily stress can exhaust your immune system, you need an energetic solution to balance and stimulate immunity. Green calcite is ideal for this purpose.

DESIRE STONE—AMETHYST

Amethyst is ideal for this grid because it's a stress-reduction crystal that can also help produce better sleep. Both are essential when you're trying to heal and strengthen your immune system.

DIRECTIONAL STONE—CLEAR QUARTZ

Clear quartz is one of the best crystals for strengthening overall health. It also amplifies and directs the energy of both the green calcite and the amethyst. Place the points so the flat ends are positioned inward toward the grid. The terminated ends should point out into the room.

TIP TO EXPAND YOUR PRACTICE

Place this grid beneath or next to your bed. You can also diffuse lavender essential oil as you sleep to boost immunity. Each night before you go to sleep, state aloud or silently, "I give thanks for my strong and healthy immune system."

ALTERNATE CRYSTAL OPTIONS

Focus stone: Moss agate
Desire stone: Chalcedony
Directional stone: Snowflake obsidian

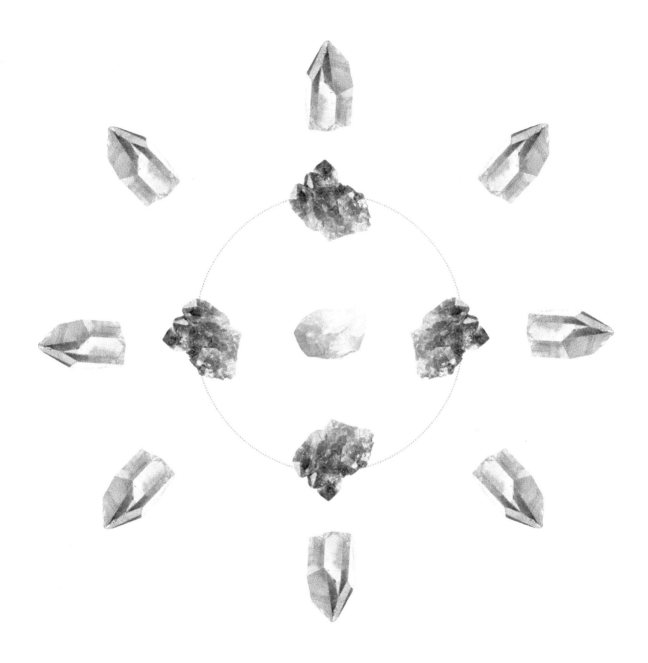

AUTOIMMUNE CONDITIONS

Shape: Spiral
Type: Balancing, Grounding, and Absorbing

Autoimmune conditions occur when the body starts to recognize its own tissue as a foreign invader and fights against it. Celiac disease, multiple sclerosis, and Graves' disease are a few examples. Gridwork with the appropriate stones can absorb excess energy and restore balance.

FOCUS STONE—BLACK TOURMALINE

The focus stone for autoimmune conditions is black tourmaline because the root chakra is where autoimmune disorders originate; in addition, it's a grounding crystal that absorbs excess immune energy.

DESIRE STONE—VARIES BASED ON CONDITION

To select a desire stone, determine where the condition affects your body the most. Choose a crystal with a color that corresponds with the chakra nearest to that body part. For skin, muscles, or skeleton, choose the stone for the crown chakra.

Root: Garnet
Sacral: Carnelian
Solar plexus: Citrine
Heart: Peridot
Throat: Chalcedony
Third eye: Amethyst
Crown: Selenite

DIRECTIONAL STONE—CLEAR QUARTZ

Clear quartz amplifies and directs the energy of the other stones in your grid. Here, you'll alternate clear quartz with your chosen desire stone in your spiral. Start with the focus stone of black tourmaline in the center and then spiral out with alternating desire stones and clear quartz, as far as you wish.

TIP TO EXPAND YOUR PRACTICE

Place the grid in your meditation space and make sure to sit on the ground next to it every day. Visualize growing roots from the base of your spine and stretching into the earth beneath you. Visualize the excess energy moving to your roots and into the earth. I do this every day for five minutes, and picture my excess energy as a grayish mist or shadow.

ALTERNATE CRYSTAL OPTIONS

Focus stone: Hematite
Desire stone: Any stone with the color of the relevant chakra
Directional stone: Selenite

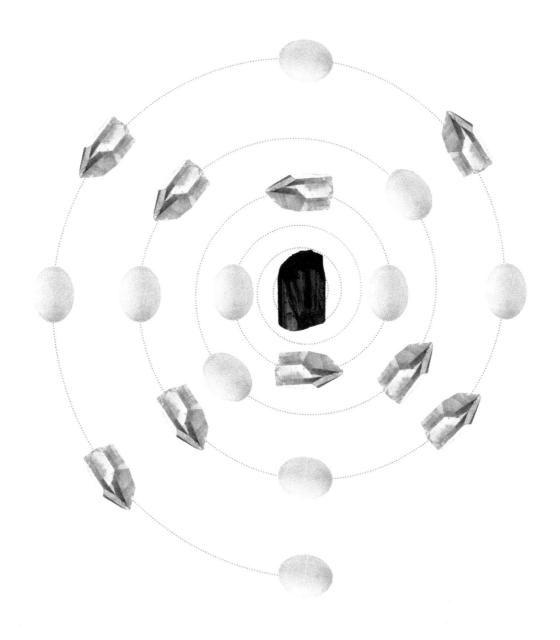

HEADACHES

Shape: *Circle*
Type: *Absorbing*

Experts believe that migraines occur when the blood vessels in the head dilate and cause blood to rush to the site, resulting in pain. Opaque crystals can absorb this excess energy. The shape of this grid is a very simple circle, because constructing anything more complex can be difficult when you're struggling with severe head pain.

FOCUS STONE—LEPIDOLITE

Lepidolite is an opaque purple crystal; it works with the energy of the third eye, which is where migraines often originate. Along with placing a grid in the bedroom where you will lie down when you have a migraine, I also recommend placing a piece of lepidolite directly on your third eye to absorb the energy.

DESIRE STONE—SNOWFLAKE OBSIDIAN

With its opacity, snowflake obsidian absorbs excess energy. The white color balances the crown chakra, while the black color balances the root chakra and grounds energy. The two colors coexisting in one stone can help send energy between the root and crown chakras.

Therefore, it will absorb any excess energy coming from the crown chakra that might contribute to the headache, while also sending the excess energy through your root chakra and into the earth to be absorbed and neutralized.

DIRECTIONAL STONE—BLACK TOURMALINE (OPTIONAL)

It's not necessary to use a third stone. However, if you'd like to further ground and absorb any energy contributing to the headache, you can create a perimeter of pieces of black tourmaline.

TIP TO EXPAND YOUR PRACTICE

I have found binaural beats to be extremely helpful for headaches. You can listen to them using headphones. I use an app called Pain Killer 2.0 on my iPhone. I stick in my earbuds, go into a dark room, and listen to it for 10 minutes. It's available both on Google Play and in the Apple Store.

ALTERNATE CRYSTAL OPTIONS

Focus stone: Chevron amethyst
Desire stone: Howlite
Directional stone: Garnet

WEIGHT LOSS

Shape: Sunburst
Type: Energizing

Weight loss is one of my students' most common physical health issues. I've struggled with weight for much of my life, in part because of a thyroid condition, and in part because I really like food. While loving and appreciating your body—no matter its shape or size—is essential, I also understand the desire to reach a certain clothing size. This weight loss grid addresses several factors that contribute to a healthy weight: self-esteem, physical appetite, metabolism, and self-compassion.

FOCUS STONE—CITRINE

For this grid, citrine strengthens your will-power and increases self-esteem and personal boundaries. You may wish to rearrange the stones based on which issue is most pressing. If willpower is an issue, it's best to make citrine the focus stone. If it's appetite, make carnelian the focus stone. If you carry a lack of self-compassion, then move rose quartz to the center.

DESIRE STONE—CARNELIAN

Carnelian is an excellent stone for absorbing and reducing excess appetite. It can also help you recognize if your desire to lose weight is something you truly want or if it is rooted in a desire to have others approve of you. The desire stones should make a circular ring around the focus stone.

DIRECTIONAL STONE—ROSE QUARTZ

Rose quartz will help you be more loving to yourself, and self-compassion is a key element of weight loss. Use the directional stones like rays of the sun, positioning them so they point outward into the room.

TIP TO EXPAND YOUR PRACTICE

The kitchen, dining room, or bathroom are all good locations for this grid. Sit near your grid, close your eyes, and visualize yourself living at your new weight. Notice how you feel, how you move, what you wear, and more. Make this visualization as vivid as you possibly can.

ALTERNATE CRYSTAL OPTIONS

Focus stone: Pyrite
Desire stone: Amber
Directional stone: Kunzite

DEPRESSION

Shape: Sunburst
Type: Energizing

Over the years, I've noticed that many of my friends and family members suffering from depression feel an associated sense of shame. Depression can arise from a chemical imbalance or it may be circumstantial, and either way, it's no more shameful than any other illness. If you're struggling with depression or other forms of mental illness, I recommend a strong dose of self-compassion and kindness as you nurture yourself deeply.

FOCUS STONE—GARNET

The root chakra is the primary energy center associated with depression. Garnet can strengthen this chakra while also helping you remain grounded and focused on the present moment. Choose a deep red rather than a green or an orange garnet. The deeper the red, the better.

DESIRE STONE—CARNELIAN AND CITRINE

Carnelian is one of my favorite crystals for focusing on positive feelings. Its sunny orange color can support optimism and help strengthen your sense of self so that you don't lose yourself in the depression. Citrine can help strengthen personal boundaries. For the desire stone, create a circle around the focus stone, alternating pieces of carnelian and citrine.

DIRECTIONAL STONE—ROSE QUARTZ

Rose quartz helps you remain rooted in compassion as you work through your depression. It can facilitate kindness and forgiveness toward yourself or others. Place the rose quartz around the ring of citrine and carnelian so that the pieces point outward like rays of the sun.

TIP TO EXPAND YOUR PRACTICE

If your depression is associated with grief, I recommend incorporating Apache tears into your grid layout. These are rounded obsidian stones and are effective at processing grief. Create an inner circle of Apache tears around the center garnet stone and inside of the carnelian and citrine.

ALTERNATE CRYSTAL OPTIONS

Focus stone: Hematite
Desire stone: Amber
Directional stone: Kunzite

ANXIETY

Shape: *Triquetra*
Type: *Calming and Grounding*

As an empath, I experience the emotions and physical sensations of others as if they are my own. This is a condition I have learned to manage, but in large groups, it can feel bombarding. This can lead to high anxiety during social events and a strong need to decompress afterward. I use this triquetra grid to help manage that anxiety and calm myself when it arises.

FOCUS STONE—LEPIDOLITE

Lepidolite contains lithium, which is a chemical that increases serotonin levels in the brain. The properties of the lithium in the lepidolite make it a highly effective stone for anxiety; if you suffer from an anxiety disorder, I strongly recommend trying to find lepidolite online if it's not available locally.

DESIRE STONE—BLUE LACE AGATE AND RAINBOW FLUORITE

Blue lace agate is one of the most calming stones you can find. Its lovely blue color brings peace and absorbs anxiety. If you have an anxiety disorder, I recommend keeping a piece of it with you. Rainbow fluorite also absorbs anxiety. You can use one or both of these. If you use both, alternate them in the desire stone layer.

DIRECTIONAL STONE—BLACK TOURMALINE

Often, a lack of grounding can lead to anxiety. Black tourmaline can help. Create a circle of black tourmaline around the triquetra. This grounds energy and helps you feel more solidly connected to the earth.

TIP TO EXPAND YOUR PRACTICE

Chamomile flowers or dried lavender flowers are excellent for soothing anxiety and are often used in tea for that purpose. Alternate the flowers with the desire crystals or place them in a ring around the outer circle of directional stones.

ALTERNATE CRYSTAL OPTIONS

Focus stone: Turquoise
Desire stone: Chalcedony
Directional stone: Smoky quartz

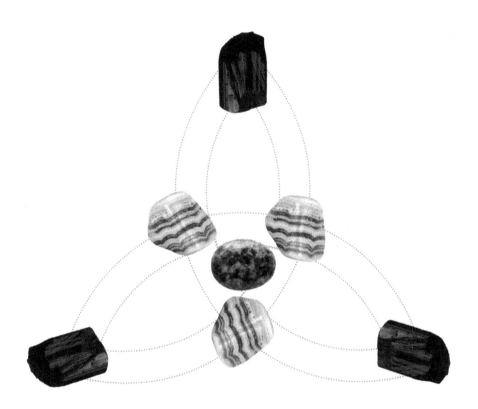

ALLERGIES

*Shape: Inverted Triangle with a line
(Earth symbol)*
Type: Absorbing and Grounding

People who have allergies tend to have an imbalance of the Ayurvedic elements of Earth, Air, Fire, Water, and Ether. In particular, people with allergies sometimes have an overabundance of Air and Ether. A grounding earth triangle grid can help balance excess Air and Ether.

Note: If you are deathly allergic to something and risk anaphylaxis, do not rely on a crystal grid to make it safe to consume that substance, and always keep an EpiPen handy.

FOCUS STONE—CARNELIAN

Carnelian can calm overreactions within your immune system. It can also strengthen your solar plexus and root chakra regions, particularly if you find a piece that's a deep red-orange as opposed to a lighter orange.

DESIRE STONE—GREEN CALCITE

Allergies tend to affect your lungs and manifest as respiratory distress, and the lungs are governed by the heart chakra. Green calcite is a heart chakra crystal that can help absorb the overactive energy of the respiratory system when you suffer a mild allergic reaction.

DIRECTIONAL STONE—CLEAR QUARTZ

Clear quartz is the best stone to support overall health. You can place the clear quartz in a circle around the inverted triangle to magnify the healing properties of the calcite and carnelian and to protect your general physical health.

TIP TO EXPAND YOUR PRACTICE

Practice gratitude for your body as it attempts to protect you from what it perceives as a dangerous substance. Give thanks daily to your body for all it does to keep you safe and protected. I make gratitude and words of affirmation for my body a daily ritual when I meditate.

ALTERNATE CRYSTAL OPTIONS

Focus stone: Amber or peach moonstone
Desire stone: Malachite
Directional stone: Snowflake obsidian

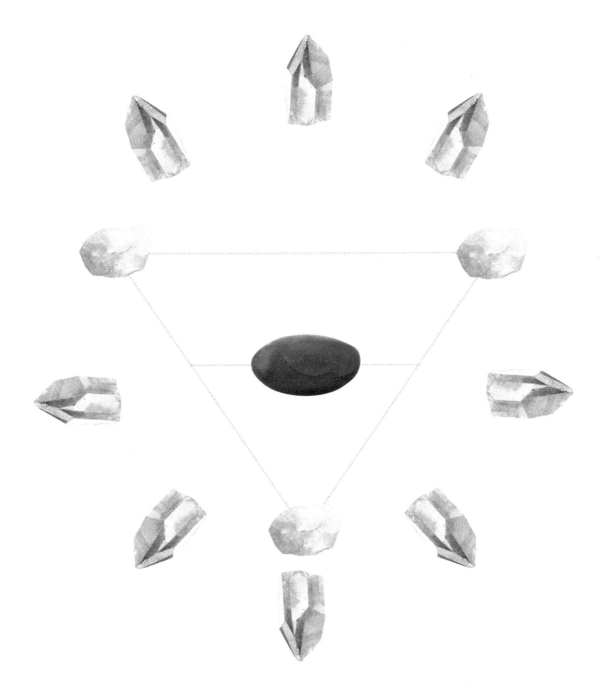

HEART HEALTH

Shape: Triquetra
Type: Strengthening and Balancing

There are a number of energies that can contribute to poor heart health. Anger, stress, bitterness, and unexpressed pain are all examples of emotions that, when suppressed, get buried in your body and weaken your heart. Numerous studies have shown the connection between stress, heart disease, and inflammation, which is also an increased risk factor for heart disease. This grid can help release the risk factors associated with coronary disease.

FOCUS STONE—PERIDOT

Peridot is a heart chakra stone. It can help balance the energy of the heart and also provide spiritual and emotional equilibrium, allowing you to release negative and stressful emotions that can damage your heart over the long term.

DESIRE STONE—RAINBOW FLUORITE

Rainbow fluorite is beneficial for heart health and alleviating stress. It can help calm bitterness or rage and bring about kinder and more forgiving emotions that are beneficial to your overall health.

DIRECTIONAL STONE—GARNET

Garnet is a stone that can help improve circulation health, which is essential for combating high blood pressure and coronary artery disease. Create a circle of garnet around the outside of your Celtic knot.

TIP TO EXPAND YOUR PRACTICE

Sit near your grid and close your eyes. Place both hands over your heart. Visualize a ball of pink, warm light growing in your chest and think about something that makes you feel deep love—a significant other, a grandparent, a pet, a child. Visualize the ball of pink light growing under your hands with each heartbeat. See it expand throughout your body, radiating into every cell. Watch it flow out of your skin into the universe. Sit bathed in the pink light for five minutes.

ALTERNATE CRYSTAL OPTIONS

Focus stone: Malachite
Desire stone: Chalcedony
Directional stone: Kunzite

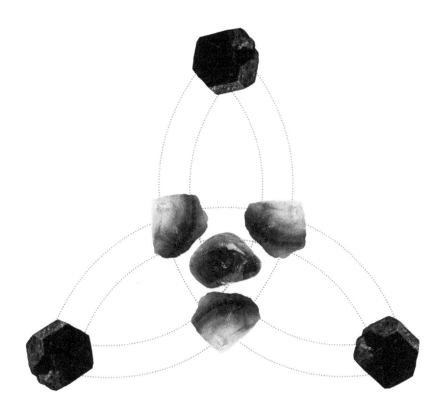

BETTER SLEEP

Shape: Triskelion
Type: Relaxing and Releasing

I used to be a terrible sleeper; I'd lay awake for hours with my mind running wild. I started to create grids in my bedroom, on my nightstand, and would reset them every couple of days. Since then, I sleep better and for longer periods of time. The triskelion shape can help you focus on the now, which helps calm your busy mind.

FOCUS STONE—AMETHYST

Amethyst is a fabulous sleep stone. Even when I don't have a grid set up in my room, I keep amethyst clusters on both bedside tables as well as on my dresser. When I travel and forget to bring amethyst along, I don't sleep as well. If you have sleep issues, amethyst is a must-have (which is why I don't recommend a replacement focus stone for this particular grid layout). A small piece will help, but a small cluster is an even better choice.

DESIRE STONE—MOONSTONE

With a name like moonstone, is it any surprise that this crystal can help you sleep well? Its calming energy soothes the mind and allows you to gently drift off to sleep. It can also help increase the depth and quality of your sleep.

DIRECTIONAL STONE—LEPIDOLITE

Lepidolite helps release stress and anxiety. From my own personal experience with insomnia, I discovered that anxiety about whether I was actually going to be able to go to sleep worsened my inability to sleep. Likewise, worries that sometimes arise during the night can often contribute to poor sleep. If one of the reasons you're struggling to sleep is anxiety, then lepidolite is your stone.

TIP TO EXPAND YOUR PRACTICE

Every night before bed I also repeat the following mantra: "I sleep deeply, soundly, peacefully, and comfortably, and I awake feeling vibrant and refreshed." Try coming up with your own sleep mantra to repeat each night and affirm it before you go to bed. You can also write this on a piece of paper, fold it up, and place it under your focus stone.

ALTERNATE CRYSTAL OPTIONS

Desire stone: Labradorite
Directional stone: Selenite

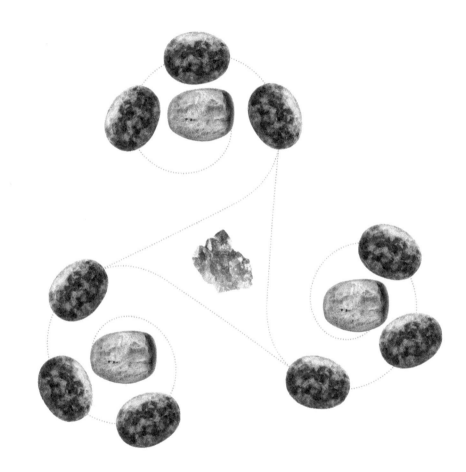

STRESS AND RELAXATION

Shape: *Triquetra*
Type: *Relaxing and Releasing*

Stress affects every aspect of health, from the foods you eat to how well you sleep and how well your immune system functions. It's essential to your mental, physical, and spiritual well-being that you learn to manage stress and find ways to relax. This grid can help.

FOCUS STONE—CHALCEDONY

Chalcedony is a beautifully calming stone. Its peaceful blue color facilitates relaxation and encourages stress release. It can also help relieve depression, anger, anxiety, and other issues that deepen stress.

DESIRE STONE—ROSE QUARTZ

Rose quartz strengthens your adrenal glands, which can become exhausted if you experience chronic stress. Adrenal glands that work around the clock diminish your ability to handle stress, so strengthening them is essential.

DIRECTIONAL STONE—CELESTITE

The peaceful blue of celestite can also help calm stress and induce relaxation. It's an excellent stone for relieving anxiety and calming persistent thought patterns that contribute to stress, such as worry or unreleased anger.

TIP TO EXPAND YOUR PRACTICE

This is a beautiful blue and pink grid; the crystals relieve stress, and the colors promote a calming atmosphere. Add a circle of lavender flowers around your grid and diffuse lavender essential oil to further release stress and promote relaxation.

ALTERNATE CRYSTAL OPTIONS

Focus stone: Blue lace agate
Desire stone: Kunzite
Directional stone: Tanzanite

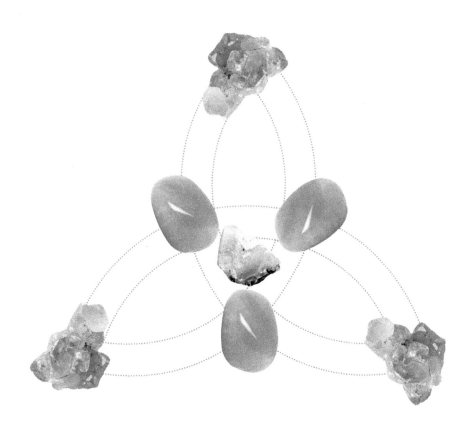

CHAPTER 6

Realize Your Creative Expression

THE VERY NATURE OF LIFE is creativity. Every act you undertake is a creative one, even if it feels mundane. Likewise, every thought and word has creative potential.

Many people express to me that while they have creative ideas, they often don't bring them to fruition. And while not every creative thought needs to turn into physical reality, if there's a significant disconnect between creative ideas and their expression, there's probably also an energetic imbalance.

Creativity originates in the sacral, or second, chakra. Inspiration for creativity also comes from a higher source, such as your higher self, in dreams, or even from the Divine itself. These ideas exist to help you serve your greatest good or to support the highest good of the universe as a whole.

The grids in this chapter support all of these elements of creativity, helping you to discover both ideation and expression in ways that will best serve you throughout your life.

CREATIVE DREAMING

Shape: *Seed of Life*
Type: *Guidance*

Dreams are a valuable source of creative inspiration. Ideas for several of my creative projects, including inspiration for the books that I write and the classes I teach, have come to me in dreams. I believe this happens because it's easiest for our higher selves and spirit guides to communicate with us when we are in this relaxed and clear state.

FOCUS STONE—AMETHYST

In my dream interpretation classes, I tell my students that if they want to spark intuition and receive guidance while they sleep, amethyst is the best stone to facilitate this. It is a stone of intuition and a crystal for dreamers.

DESIRE STONE—MOONSTONE

Many people believe they don't dream, but the fact is that we all do—sometimes it's just more difficult to remember the content and details of our dreams. This is where moonstone comes in. It connects your subconscious mind to your conscious mind, improving your recollection of dreams and helping you bring their creative inspiration into your waking life.

DIRECTIONAL STONE—CLEAR QUARTZ

Clear quartz can help with problem solving, and dreams are the prime time to come up with creative solutions. Clear quartz can connect you to Divine guidance and amplify any messages you receive in your dreams. Use any form of clear quartz here; it doesn't need to be quartz points.

TIP TO EXPAND YOUR PRACTICE

Ask for creative dreams before you sleep. If you're working on something specific, write down the problem you're trying to solve on a piece of paper and place it under your pillow. Put the grid either under your bed or on your bedside table. Then, as you drift off to sleep, ask, either aloud or in your head, for a solution to the problem you've written on the paper.

ALTERNATE CRYSTAL OPTIONS

Focus stone: Lepidolite or rainbow fluorite
Desire stone: Selenite
Directional stone: Snowflake obsidian

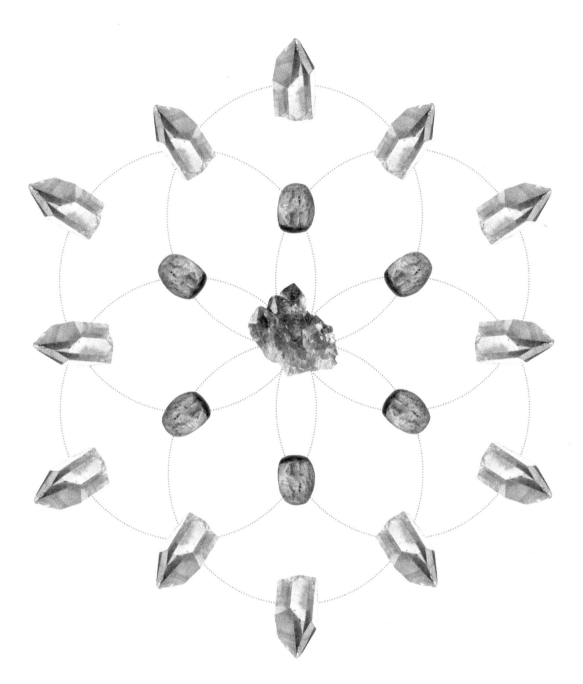

CREATIVE INSPIRATION

Shape: Vesica piscis
Type: Inspiration

My work as a writer and teacher is highly creative in nature. I often maintain a crystal grid in my workspace when I'm midproject to keep inspiration and ideas flowing. The vesica piscis is the ideal simple grid to help you gain inspiration anytime you need to get your creativity flowing.

FOCUS STONE—CARNELIAN

Creative ideas form in the midst of clear and active sacral chakra energy. Carnelian is a stone that balances and stimulates the sacral chakra and can help spark creative ideas and allow them to germinate.

DESIRE STONE—CHALCEDONY

Chalcedony, especially the deeper blue color, stimulates the third eye and throat chakras, which are the sources of Divine inspiration (third eye) and creative expression (throat chakra). It's perfect to help you receive Divine guidance in the form of creative ideas while also allowing you to freely express yourself creatively once the ideas form.

DIRECTIONAL STONE—SMOKY QUARTZ (OPTIONAL)

Directional stones aren't necessary for this grid. However, if you'd like to add an additional layer to your grid, smoky quartz can transmute all energy to positivity. This can help you feel safe and comfortable as you explore your creativity.

TIP TO EXPAND YOUR PRACTICE

Creativity comes from intuition. When you ignore creative ideas or don't act on them, you send a message to your intuition that you don't desire or need them. Therefore, it's important to always acknowledge creative ideas, even if they only come in quick flashes. Keep a small journal to record when inspiration strikes. A few times a week, go through your creative ideas and act on those you feel compelled to complete.

ALTERNATE CRYSTAL OPTIONS

Focus stone: Ametrine
Desire stone: Tanzanite
Directional stone: Citrine

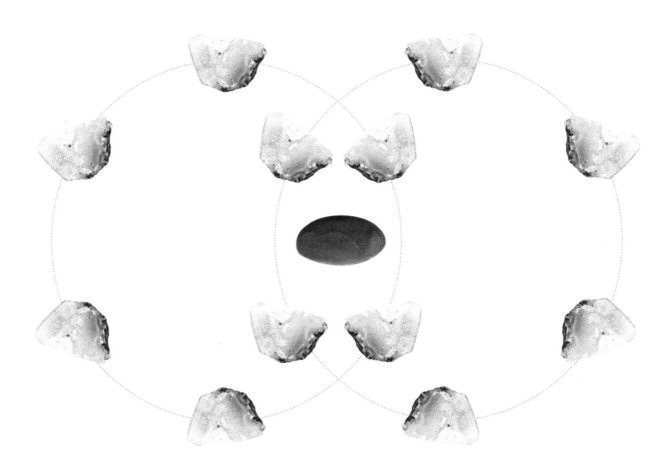

EXPRESSING CREATIVE IDEAS

Shape: *Pentagram*
Type: *Expanding*

Creative expression requires a balance between your sacral chakra, where creative ideas are born, and your throat chakra, where that creativity is expressed. To fully realize your creative potential, you'll need to strengthen the solar plexus chakra for confident self-expression and the heart chakra to ignite a passion for your creation.

FOCUS STONE—AMETRINE

Ametrine is a combination of citrine and amethyst growing together in the same stone. I love this stone because it connects higher guidance from your third eye chakra and allows it to fuel your self-confidence in your solar plexus chakra.

DESIRE STONE—CARNELIAN AND LABRADORITE

Add carnelian to stimulate creativity in your solar plexus chakra. The carnelian lets the universe know that you are ready and open for creative inspiration. Labradorite stimulates the throat chakra and fuels self-expression. Put the carnelian in the center of the pentagram around the focus stone and then use the labradorite to create the points of the pentagram.

DIRECTIONAL STONE—RAINBOW FLUORITE

Place the rainbow fluorite in a ring around the outside of the pentagram. Rainbow fluorite has colors that connect all of the disparate energies required for creative energy, from your sacral chakra, through your solar plexus and heart, and into your throat. The purple shades draw the inspirational energy from your third eye down into your throat for self-expression.

TIP TO EXPAND YOUR PRACTICE

Place your grid in your meditation space. Lie next to your grid and place a piece of carnelian on your sacral chakra—just below your belly button—and a piece of labradorite on your throat. Close your eyes and relax for five to ten minutes, visualizing energy rising from the carnelian and flowing through the labradorite and out of you into the universe.

ALTERNATE CRYSTAL OPTIONS

Focus stone: Iolite sunstone
Desire stone: Citrine
Directional stone: Amethyst

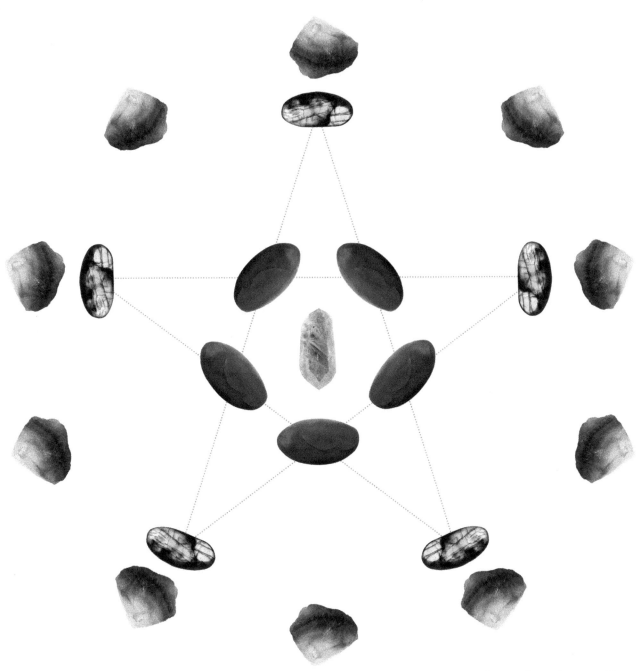

PERFORMANCE AND PUBLIC SPEAKING

Shape: Lotus
Type: Balancing

Performance always involves putting your creativity out into the world for others to see. I'm a musician, and I do a lot of public speaking, but both experiences used to give me a lot of anxiety. Fear of public speaking and performance can cause enormous stress for many people. This grid can help calm that fear and allow you to express yourself clearly through performance.

FOCUS STONE—TURQUOISE

Turquoise can help you communicate clearly and express yourself truthfully. Being able to do this for all kinds of performances, whether you're playing music for a crowd, acting in a play, or speaking at a conference, is essential. This stone can also calm and reduce anxiety.

DESIRE STONE—PYRITE

To the next layer, add pyrite for charisma. With its glittery gold exterior, pyrite will both fire you up and help you present your creative ideas with confidence and power, which will boost your performance.

DIRECTIONAL STONE—BLACK TOURMALINE

When you're performing, being grounded and present in your body is essential to delivering a great performance, whether it's dance, theater, music, or speech. When I'm not grounded, I often forget what I was saying in the middle of a talk. Reconnecting to the planet with black tourmaline helps prevent such occurences.

TIP TO EXPAND YOUR PRACTICE

Meditate next to your grid in the days leading up to your performance for five to ten minutes at a time. As you meditate, visualize everything going flawlessly and the audience responding positively to the message you are sending through your performance.

ALTERNATE CRYSTAL OPTIONS

Focus stone: Sodalite or lapis lazuli
Desire stone: Yellow tiger's-eye
Directional stone: Garnet

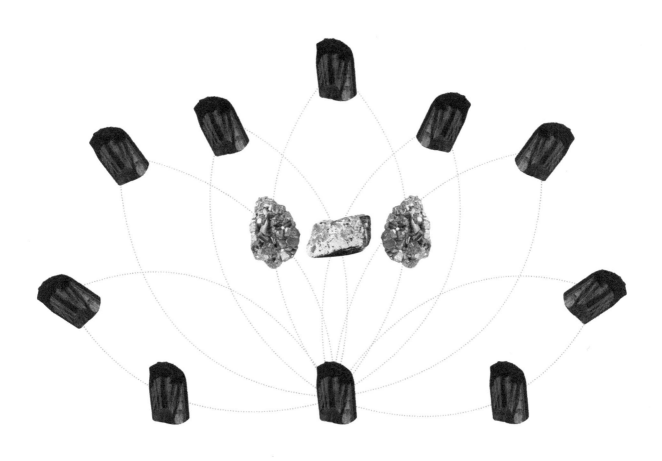

WRITING

Shape: *Triangle (upright, no line)*
Type: *Expanding*

Writing is something everyone can do. It's a great way to share your creative ideas, even if it's writing letters or journaling. Before I worked as a writer, I still expressed my creativity through the written word. It doesn't require any special equipment or know-how to do, but it does take a certain level of clarity of thought, creative inspiration, and communication ability. If you have a place to sit and write, whether at work or in a home office or studio, set up this simple writing grid nearby.

FOCUS STONE—CARNELIAN

You'll find carnelian as the focus stone of many creativity grids because it is such a powerful force for inspiring and developing creative ideas. Place the carnelian directly in the center of your triangle to attract creative ideas.

DESIRE STONE—MOONSTONE AND LABRADORITE

For the outer layer of the triangle, place moonstones on each of the points of the triangle and a piece of labradorite in the center of each of the lines that makes up the triangle. Moonstone will help you develop patience and perseverance as you write, while labradorite will facilitate expression through writing.

DIRECTIONAL STONE—AMETHYST

Place a circle of amethyst stones around the outside of the triangle to complete the grid. Amethyst will help keep you calm while also connecting your ideas and Divine inspiration with written expression.

TIP TO EXPAND YOUR PRACTICE

For large outdoor grids, drawing them with chalk or tracing a path in the dirt is ideal because it helps guide crystal placement. For smaller grids you can use grid cloths, print outlines from the internet, or even copy the grid outlines included in this book onto a piece of paper. Alternatively, you can freehand the grids since intention is more important than precision.

ALTERNATE CRYSTAL OPTIONS

Focus stone: Amber or sunstone
Desire stone: Turquoise
Directional stone: Lepidolite

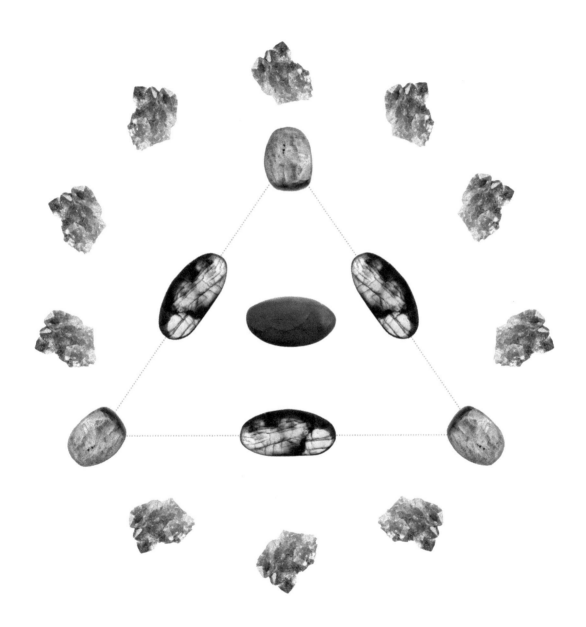

MUSIC

Shape: *Triskelion*
Type: *Expressing*

Music is a great way to express yourself, whether you like to sing in the shower, play an instrument, or just listen to music that inspires you. Even if you aren't a musician, you can still seek creative expression through the act of listening to music and feeling it flow through you.

FOCUS STONE—AMETRINE

The focus stone of ametrine serves two purposes here: It offers inspiration for making music a part of your life, and it gives you the courage and confidence to express yourself musically. That might involve dancing to music, belting out a tune the next time you're in the car, or performing in front of an audience.

DESIRE STONE—SMOKY QUARTZ

Smoky quartz sparks creative ideas and helps you feel more positive about expressing yourself musically. It can also boost your self-confidence, which can ease performance anxiety.

DIRECTIONAL STONE—CELESTITE

If you're a singer or play a wind instrument, celestite will strengthen your vocal cords and help with your throat and breath support. Even if you don't sing or play a wind instrument, celestite will strengthen your ability to express your truth through music in any way you choose.

TIP TO EXPAND YOUR PRACTICE

If you enjoy music but don't prefer it as a form of creative expression, you can still bring its creative energy into your life. To do this, sit next to your grid and put on a piece of instrumental music you really like. Close your eyes and feel the music moving deeply through your body. Notice any ideas or thoughts that come to your mind as you do this.

ALTERNATE CRYSTAL OPTIONS

Focus stone: Rainbow fluorite
Desire stone: Amber
Directional stone: Blue lace agate or sodalite

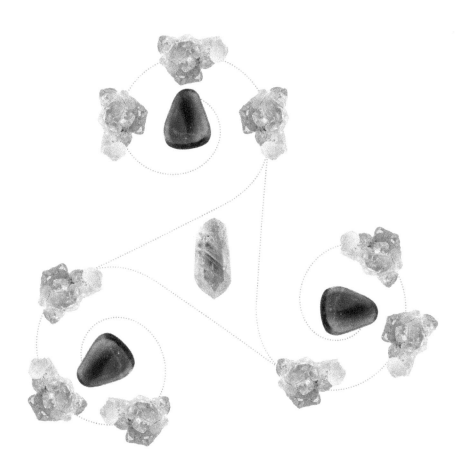

VISUAL ART

Shape: *Flower of Life or Seed of Life*
Type: *Expressing*

Visual art can take many forms: painting, sculpting, designing jewelry, sewing, crocheting, scrapbooking, drawing, and many others. Even if your ability to draw is like mine (mostly stick figures), playing with form and color is a visual and tactile type of creativity that's fun and enriching. This grid can help you express yourself visually.

FOCUS STONE—CITRINE

Citrine serves a dual purpose here: It encourages joy and can strengthen your confidence in expressing yourself through a visual medium. With its connection to your solar and sacral plexus chakras, self-confidence and creative ideas (sacral chakra) arise, respectively.

DESIRE STONE—AMETHYST

Amethyst provides inspiration from higher sources. It also connects your creative mind to your throat chakra, which is the energetic center that supports the physical part of your body that includes your hands and arms. Amethyst can strengthen and support the energy of these physical areas of your body that are often used

to create visual art. It can also strengthen Divine inspiration in creating that art.

DIRECTIONAL STONE—SODALITE

Sodalite can help with self-expression. It can also help lessen criticism and judgment—something I find I regularly apply to my own artwork. Removing or softening these two negative habits allows you to become more open to expressing yourself in the moment without worrying about the finished product. It provides you the opportunity to explore color and texture without second-guessing yourself.

TIP TO EXPAND YOUR PRACTICE

Place your grid wherever you create art or crafts. Put down some papers and grab an inexpensive canvas. Without thinking, judging, or planning, use acrylic or watercolor paints to splash colors across the canvas. The goal is to explore your personal relationship to color and form. I spent about six months doing this a few times a week, and although I didn't produce any usable paintings, it really sparked my creativity and brought me the joy of self-expression.

ALTERNATE CRYSTAL OPTIONS

Focus stone: Amber
Desire stone: Ametrine or lepidolite
Directional stone: Chalcedony

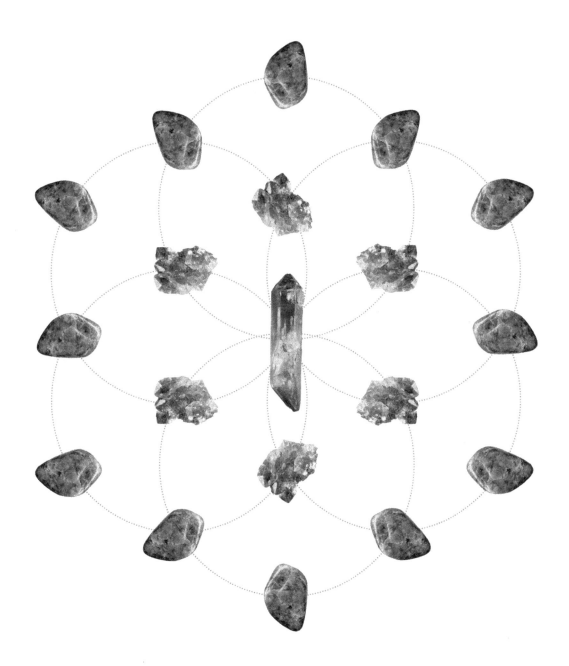

SHARING YOUR CREATIVE TRUTH

Shape: Triquetra
Type: Expressing

As embodied humans living in polite society, we've often learned to clamp down on our truth and keep it to ourselves. If you don't abide by this, you may be accused of self-aggrandizing or risk hurting someone's feelings. Sharing and living your truth is one of the most important things you can do for your own well-being. This grid is designed to help you express your truth through whatever creative outlet you choose.

FOCUS STONE—SODALITE

Placing sodalite as the focus stone in this grid serves multiple purposes. It softens or removes judgment and criticism toward oneself and others, which is essential in truth-speaking. It also facilitates honest discourse and self-expression, and it boosts your ability to come from a place of integrity while still retaining diplomacy.

DESIRE STONE—AMBER

Amber has a warm energy that sparks creativity while helping you remain in a place of confidence in your own beliefs, ideas, and thoughts. A darker amber supports the energy of creative ideas, whereas a lighter-colored amber supports the energy of self-confidence. You can even alternate between dark- and light-colored amber if you need to support both energies, such as when you aren't feeling confident in your creativity.

DIRECTIONAL STONE—ROSE QUARTZ

Rose quartz allows you to express your truth from a place of self-love, compassion, kindness, and care for others. It can help soften the truth you want to express but still encourage you to be lovingly honest.

TIP TO EXPAND YOUR PRACTICE

Even if you're uncomfortable expressing your truth to others, it is essential to be truthful with yourself. In developing self-trust, you'll become more comfortable living your truth around other people as well. Write truths about yourself on small pieces of paper. Fold them up and place one under each of the rose quartz stones on the grid.

ALTERNATE CRYSTAL OPTIONS

Focus stone: Celestite or lapis lazuli
Desire stone: Carnelian
Directional stone: Kunzite or peridot

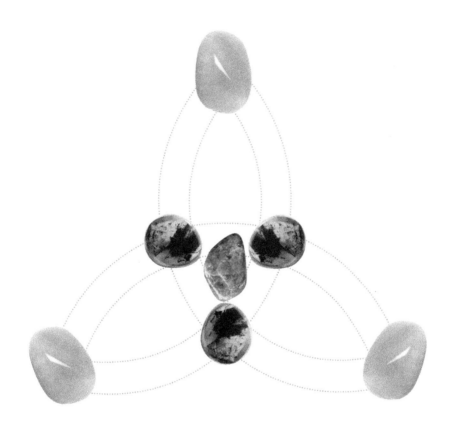

FOLLOWING YOUR CREATIVE PATH

Shape: *Spiral*
Type: *Directing*

Spiral grids represent the unfolding of a path. I tell my students that walking a spiritual path is the ultimate act of creation. This is a powerful grid that supports the creation of your own spiritual and personal path in this lifetime as a soul living in a human body.

FOCUS STONE—LEPIDOLITE

Place lepidolite at the center of your spiral. This will help spark guidance from your higher self or your spirit guides about the creative spiritual path that will serve your greatest good. You can also use additional pieces of lepidolite as the spiral opens, if you wish, alternating it with the other stones in the grid.

DESIRE STONE—TURQUOISE AND SELENITE

Create the swirls of your spiral with alternating pieces of turquoise and selenite. Turquoise allows you to share your creative truth, while selenite connects you to the Source, which is where your soul ultimately resides. You can also alternate the turquoise and selenite with additional lepidolite, if you wish.

DIRECTIONAL STONE—SELENITE

Place a piece of selenite at the very end of your grid. This will draw Source energy into the grid, energizing it with Divine inspiration.

TIP TO EXPAND YOUR PRACTICE

The spiral is the perfect grid to build outdoors on a large scale. Use chalk to first draw the grid. Even with a huge grid, you don't need to add a whole bunch of stones—add them just as you would with a smaller grid. Once it's complete, start at the center of the spiral and walk through it until you reach the end. Take five to ten minutes, using slow steps while contemplating your creative path.

ALTERNATE CRYSTAL OPTIONS

Focus stone: Amethyst
Desire stone: Celestite
Directional stone: Clear quartz

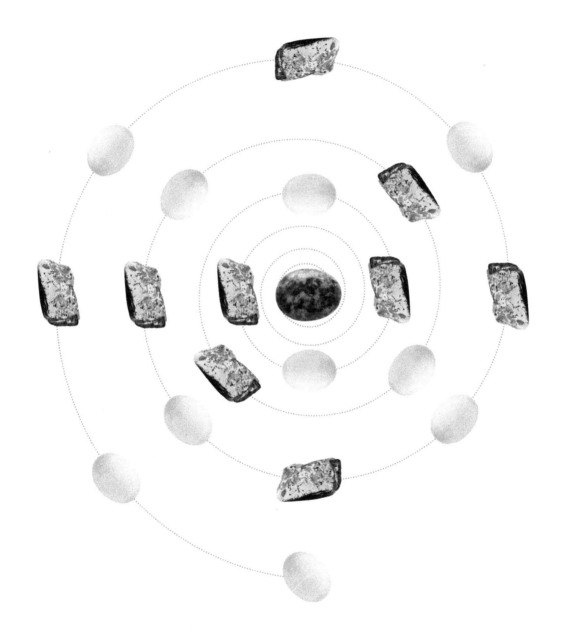

CURIOSITY AND PASSION

Shape: Sunburst
Type: Attracting

Many creative ideas start with curiosity—seeking out the answers to who, what, why, how, when, and where. Passion carries you along this path, allowing your creativity to flower and grow into something that can make your life better, help you find your true purpose, or even improve the world by serving the greatest good.

FOCUS STONE—LABRADORITE

Labradorite is an energizing stone that invites curiosity, prompting you to seek out creative ways to explore the universe and your place in it. It also allows the ideas you receive to germinate and ultimately express themselves in ways that support your soul's purpose.

DESIRE STONE—ROSE QUARTZ

In order to walk a creative path, you need to do so from a place of unconditional love for yourself, others, and the universe at large. Rose quartz is a stone of love and compassion. It purifies your creativity and ignites a spark of true, unconditional love that keeps you living and expressing the highest of intentions. Place the rose quartz stones in an inner circle around the focus stone.

DIRECTIONAL STONE—GARNET

Garnet is a stone of passion. It will give you that spark that drives you forward in your creative quest. It can also ground the creativity in your embodied self and help remove any anxiety or fear associated with creative exploration of the universe. Place garnets in a sunburst pattern around the inner ring of rose quartz.

TIP TO EXPAND YOUR PRACTICE

Add marigolds, dandelions, or another bright yellow flower to this grid. This incorporates sunny optimism and makes the grid fun to look at. Alternate flowers with the garnets to create the rays of the sunburst.

ALTERNATE CRYSTAL OPTIONS

Focus stone: Sodalite
Desire stone: Peridot or green calcite
Directional stone: Ruby or hematoid quartz

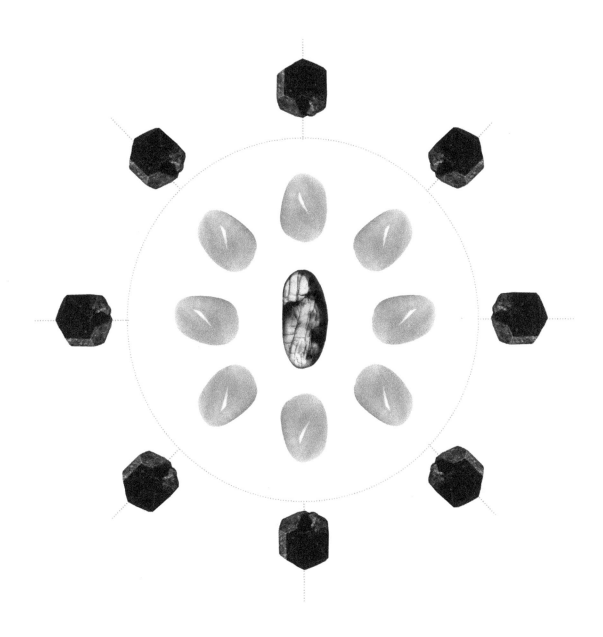

CHAPTER 7

Expand Your Career, Wealth, and Prosperity

YOUR CAREER DOESN'T ALWAYS mean the work you do for pay. It can also be your vocation or the activities you engage in with meaning as a volunteer, a hobbyist, or an entrepreneur. Wealth describes your finances, money, or things that represent money, such as investments or possessions in your life. Prosperity is defined as an abundance in all the things you desire. This can include health, wealth, friendships, love, and more.

Prosperity is usually a big hurdle for many. There are a number of reasons why people struggle with abundance, but most of them center on subconscious beliefs and attitudes related to a "consciousness of lack" (see page 5). That was certainly true for me when my son graduated from college with his BA in music. The spring semester of his high school senior year, I suddenly realized the time to pay his tuition and living expenses was nearly upon us. We didn't have money set aside for it, and I panicked. My first thought was, "There is no way we will ever be able to pay for five years of college."

I immediately went to work on my prosperity and consciousness of lack. I created crystal grids and started using affirmations and visualization daily. In the end, we seldom had to sacrifice to pay for my son's schooling.

PERSONAL WEALTH

Shape: *Triquetra*
Type: *Attracting and Magnetizing*

One of the things my clients most often ask me is how to expand personal wealth. Many people feel that wishing to accumulate wealth is a selfish value, but others may have issues surrounding wealth arising from childhood beliefs or from difficult financial periods in their lives.

FOCUS STONE—CITRINE

Citrine is the most well-known wealth and prosperity stone. I recommend keeping a piece of citrine in a business cash box or in your wallet (or both). By strengthening your solar plexus chakra, citrine can also help you overcome a negative self-image that may be blocking your prosperity.

DESIRE STONE—PYRITE

Pyrite resembles gold (so much so that it was called "fool's gold" during the Gold Rush), so it is another excellent crystal to turn you into a magnet for financial abundance. Pyrite also will absorb excess ego energy, which can help reverse any belief in your lack of abundance that might be blocking your ability to prosper.

DIRECTIONAL STONE—BLACK TOURMALINE AND CLEAR QUARTZ

Use black tourmaline to help ground the concept of wealth and abundance in the physical. The powerful grounding ability of black tourmaline allows you to anchor the concept of abundance on the earthly plane. Meanwhile, clear quartz provides amplification of prosperous energy and directs it toward you. Place the clear quartz points on the points of the triquetra, and then create a circle by placing three pieces of black tourmaline—one between each piece of clear quartz where the arc of a circle would be.

TIP TO EXPAND YOUR PRACTICE

Place your wealth grid near where you do business, such as in your office, or in the feng shui wealth sector of your home, office, or any room (see page 67). Around your grid, create an additional perimeter of Chinese coins, which are the feng shui symbol for wealth.

ALTERNATE CRYSTAL OPTIONS

Focus stone: Peridot
Desire stone: Green calcite
Directional stone: Selenite and hematite

REVERSING A CONSCIOUSNESS OF LACK

Shape: Triquetra
Type: Transmuting

For many people, the key to improving personal wealth and prosperity is overcoming the belief that there is not enough. For people who grew up in difficult financial circumstances or experienced them in early adulthood, this idea can become a stuck pattern of thinking. This grid can help reverse that pattern and let your deserved abundance flow.

FOCUS STONE—CARNELIAN

The consciousness of lack resides in the energy of our solar plexus chakra; this is where we develop and store the idea that there isn't enough to go around. Carnelian can rebalance the energy in this region to help you reverse your beliefs about abundance.

DESIRE STONE—YELLOW TIGER'S-EYE

Yellow tiger's-eye (it also comes in blue and red) strengthens self-esteem, self-worth, and personal power. Adding yellow tiger's-eye to your grid can help remove negative thoughts about deserving abundance.

DIRECTIONAL STONE—SMOKY QUARTZ

Create a ring of smoky quartz around the inner triquetra as your directional stone. You can use any form of smoky quartz you choose, as its role here is to transmute any negative thoughts, beliefs, or energy to positive thoughts, beliefs, and energy. This is another way of turning around the way you think about wealth.

TIP TO EXPAND YOUR PRACTICE

Reversing a consciousness of lack takes a lot of effort because it's usually so deeply ingrained in our psyches. So place the grid near where you spend the most time. Cleanse the stones and re-lay the grid every three to four days. At the same time, catch yourself when thoughts of "lack" arise. Immediately replace them with an affirmation such as "I give thanks to the universe that I am prosperous."

ALTERNATE CRYSTAL OPTIONS

Focus stone: Amber
Desire stone: Pyrite
Directional stone: Clear quartz

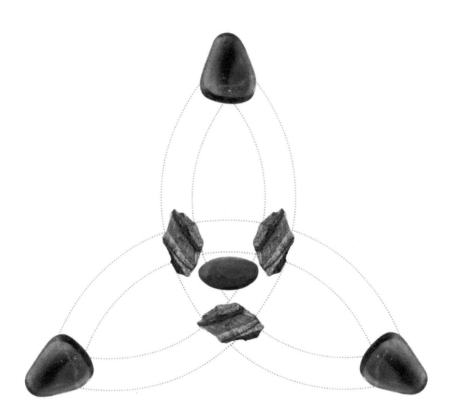

PROSPERITY CONSCIOUSNESS

Shape: *Seed of Life*
Type: *Expanding*

As you seek to dismantle your deeply held thoughts about a lack of prosperity, it's important that you simultaneously expand your consciousness of abundance—the belief that there is enough for everybody in the universe. I spent many years working with these two issues side by side, both by using crystal grids and through careful attention to the energy I put out into the universe. This grid can help you retain a consciousness of prosperity.

FOCUS STONE—AMBER

Amber is the perfect focus stone for this grid because it supports a consciousness of prosperity. It also builds self-worth to help you know that you are worthy of receiving all the gifts the universe has to offer. Placing it in the center of the seed of life allows you to sow the seeds of prosperity and nurture that consciousness as it begins to grow within you.

DESIRE STONE—CITRINE

In this case, citrine is a clear statement of desire to the universe. It is a stone of wealth, and placing it in the grid in the desire stone position tells the universe that you desire your prosperity in the form of financial abundance.

DIRECTIONAL STONE—PYRITE

The gold color of another wealth stone, pyrite, doubles down on your request to the universe that you'd like your prosperity in the form of material wealth. It can also strengthen your belief that you deserve wealth while creating positive feelings about material gain. Some people block their own wealth by feeling guilty about wanting to be wealthy. Pyrite can break this thought cycle.

TIP TO EXPAND YOUR PRACTICE

To make this grid even more powerful, place it in your office or in the feng shui wealth sector of your home. Add additional feng shui wealth symbols around the outside of the grid, such as a three-toed frog or gold-painted ingots. You can also create wealth affirmations on small pieces of paper that you fold and place under each of the crystals on your grid.

ALTERNATE CRYSTAL OPTIONS

Focus stone: Serpentine
Desire stone: Yellow tiger's-eye
Directional stone: Bismuth

CREATING A CONSCIOUSNESS OF SHARING

Shape: *Triskelion*
Type: *Joining, Magnetizing*

Sharing your gifts with others creates an energy of generosity that brings more gifts into your life as well. In order to feel safe sharing your wealth with another, you first need to feel you have enough to give away. A consciousness of sharing comes from developing compassion for others and combining it with an attitude of "there's more where that came from."

FOCUS STONE—ROSE QUARTZ

Since the foundation of sharing with others and charitable giving is made up of compassion, kindness, and unconditional love, rose quartz is the focus stone for this grid. It will center you in your heart so you have the desire to give to others and help where you are needed.

DESIRE STONE—CITRINE

Once again, citrine serves the intention of wealth in this grid. Placing citrine crystals in the desire spots tells the universe that one of the gifts you'd like to share with others is material wealth. It can also help you develop the belief that you have enough to share with others.

DIRECTIONAL STONE—CARNELIAN

Carnelian both boosts the energy of prosperity in your life and stokes the fires of generosity. Carnelian can help you choose to respond to others when you see they are in need. It can also motivate you to seek out those in need and help where you can while still respecting their dignity.

TIP TO EXPAND YOUR PRACTICE

To give, you must also learn to receive. Allowing another person to give to you is also an act of generosity because it lets that person experience their own act of selflessness. If you are someone who automatically turns down a generous offering, try spending the next month allowing yourself to receive. Accept what is being presented to you and simply say thanks. Keep a journal of your experience in receiving.

ALTERNATE CRYSTAL OPTIONS

Focus stone: Peridot or kunzite
Desire stone: Pyrite
Directional stone: Amber or sunstone

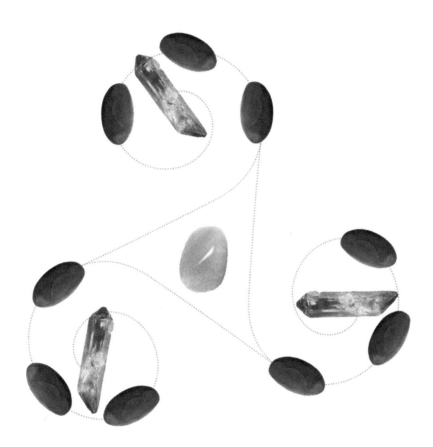

CAREER MOTIVATION

Shape: Pentagram
Type: Empowering

If you're anything like me, you've experienced varying levels of motivation throughout the life of your career. Perhaps even from day to day or hour to hour. Energize your motivation by creating an upward spiral of career growth and advancement.

FOCUS STONE—CARNELIAN

Carnelian helps your career motivation in a few different ways. First, it is a crystal that fosters and strengthens drive, so it can increase motivation. Second, it can remove any roadblocks to your success, such as fear that prevents you from moving forward or doubts about whether you will advance in your career.

DESIRE STONE—TIGER'S-EYE

Tiger's-eye helps foster self-confidence and boost your willpower. It can also help you see yourself more clearly, which will enable you to honestly assess whether your current career path suits you or whether your motivation is floundering because your career is a poor fit or doesn't serve your greatest good.

DIRECTIONAL STONE—GARNET

Using garnets anchors your newfound motivation in the physical world. Garnets can also assist with any emotional issues that are affecting your motivation and provide desire and passion to drive you forward along your career path.

TIP TO EXPAND YOUR PRACTICE

If your motivation for work continues to erode, it's time for an honest assessment of your current career path. Sit with your grid, close your eyes, and take a deep breath. Say to the universe, "Show me what I need to know about my career." Pay attention to any thoughts or feelings that arise. Do this for ten minutes per day.

ALTERNATE CRYSTAL OPTIONS

Focus stone: Amber
Desire stone: Pyrite
Directional stone: Hematoid quartz

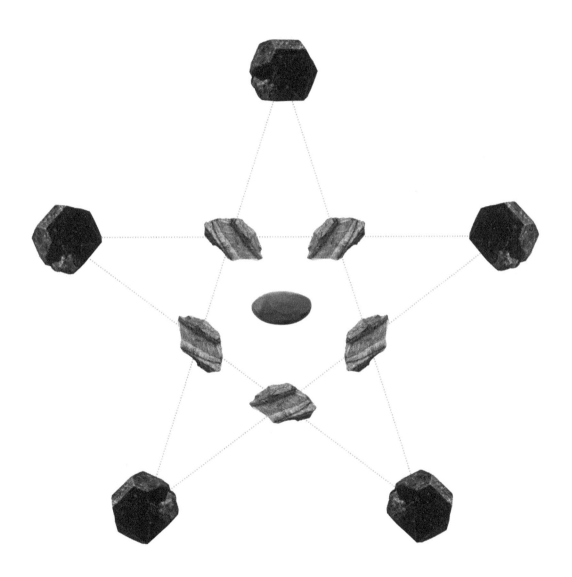

POSITIVE FOCUS

Shape: Star of David
Type: Focusing

One of the best boosts you can give your career is to come to work each day with a positive attitude and focused attention. Staying grounded in the present moment as you go about your workday enables you to feel the pleasurable aspects of a job well done. Keeping your focus on the now allows you to be present in your interactions with others at work and do your job with integrity.

FOCUS STONE—RAINBOW FLUORITE

If you need to focus on the present, rainbow fluorite is the perfect crystal to help you do so. It is a calming stone that helps you focus your mind. It also supports Divine guidance, creative problem solving, and rational thinking, which are all essential to performing well in the workplace.

DESIRE STONE—SMOKY QUARTZ

Smoky quartz helps you cultivate a positive attitude because it transmutes negative energy into positive energy—your own and that of others. This prevents any coworkers' negative attitudes from affecting yours.

DIRECTIONAL STONE—CLEAR QUARTZ

Clear quartz is used as an amplifier in this grid. It amplifies and strengthens the energy of the grid as it flows out toward you and the space you occupy. Use crystal quartz points and position the terminated (pointed) ends toward the space surrounding the grid.

TIP TO EXPAND YOUR PRACTICE

You can place this grid at your office or in the space where you get ready for work each morning. As you prepare to go to work, repeat the following affirmation: "Today is a great day at work. The work I do makes a difference in the world and satisfies me. I am excited to contribute to the greater good through my work."

ALTERNATE CRYSTAL OPTIONS

Focus stone: Blue calcite
Desire stone: Hematite
Directional stone: Snowflake obsidian

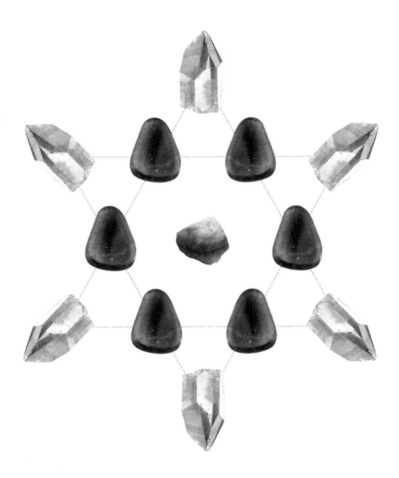

WORK ETHIC

Shape: Flower of Life
Type: Energizing

A key to success in any career is work ethic. And while part of work ethic comes from motivation (see the Career Motivation grid on page 126), some people still struggle with it for other reasons. They might believe that they are not good at their job, or maybe they work in a job they don't enjoy. Having a positive work ethic is something you can cultivate and learn regardless of what type of job you're doing. If you're in a job you don't like, you can still have a positive work ethic as you seek a position that aligns better with your needs. This grid can help strengthen your work ethic and your desire to meet or exceed expectations in the workplace.

FOCUS STONE—SNOWFLAKE OBSIDIAN

Snowflake obsidian is a great stone because it helps join the spiritual realm with the earthly plane. In terms of work ethic, that means it can help join your present attitude to the physical act of doing work. It can also help transform your thoughts and ideas into intentional acts in the workplace.

DESIRE STONE—CITRINE

In this grid, citrine represents success. It indicates to the universe that, through your focus, thoughts, and ideas, you wish to contribute to your workplace effectively. It's also an energizing yellow color to that will give you the drive to achieve peak performance at work.

DIRECTIONAL STONE—SODALITE

Sodalite can help boost your integrity, which helps you choose to do your best at work and adhere to high ethical standards. Sodalite also removes criticism and judgment so you're not wasting your work time on being self-critical or judging others.

TIP TO EXPAND YOUR PRACTICE

Write positive statements about your work on small pieces of paper. As you lay out your grid, read them aloud, then place one statement on the grid under each crystal. Each night when you come home from work, pick up the crystals and repeat the statements, replacing the crystals on top of them again or writing new statements to take their places.

ALTERNATE CRYSTAL OPTIONS

Focus stone: Moonstone
Desire stone: Pyrite
Directional stone: Labradorite

FOLLOWING YOUR PASSION

Shape: *Spiral*
Type: *Expanding*

Even though I've had multiple careers throughout my life, I've always found something to be passionate about at each job. This grid is designed to ignite your passion in the job you're currently doing or to find a job that serves your greatest good.

FOCUS STONE—GARNET

Since the key to this grid is passion, the focus stone of a red garnet communicates to the universe that you are choosing to find joy in what you do. Your desire for purpose in the workplace sends a powerful message into the universe that you choose to do exciting and meaningful work.

DESIRE STONE—YELLOW TIGER'S-EYE AND CARNELIAN

Using yellow tiger's-eye as the desire stone tells the universe that you wish to be passionate and self-directed in your work. It's a stone of power, so it indicates that you are seeking authentic personal empowerment through your career. Carnelian is a stone of courage and motivation—essential parts of passion. In the spiral, use the garnet as the focus stone, and then alternate yellow tiger's-eye, carnelian, and garnet as the grid spirals outward.

DIRECTIONAL STONE—CLEAR QUARTZ

Finish the grid with a clear quartz point at the end of the spiral, with the termination pointed outward into the universe. This will amplify the intention and send it out toward you and the space you occupy.

TIP TO EXPAND YOUR PRACTICE

The best place for this grid is in your office or in the feng shui career sector of your home (page 67). Gather small objects or images that represent what you're passionate about in your work. As a musician, I'd consider cutting out musical notes from sheet music. Place these items in your spiral grid to separate the layers.

ALTERNATE CRYSTAL OPTIONS

Focus stone: Red aventurine or fire opal
Desire stone: Pyrite, sunstone
Directional stone: Selenite

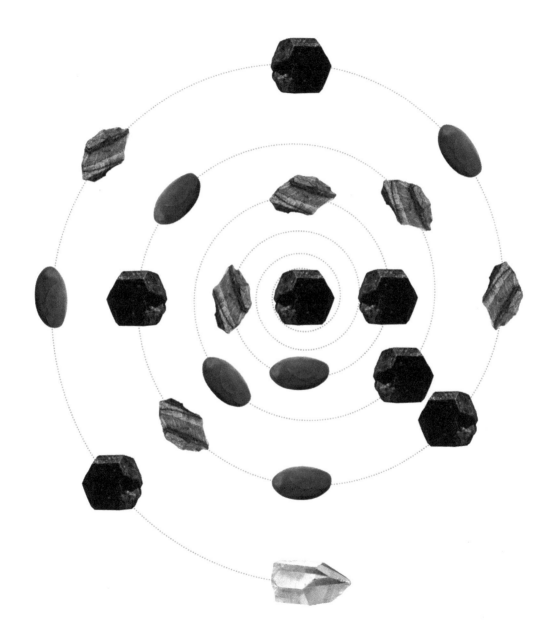

CHAPTER 8

Deepen Your Emotional Connection

YOU ARE BODY, MIND, AND SPIRIT. You cannot separate one from the others. Many of us have been taught to express only positive emotions. However, part of the human experience entails experiencing every emotion—positive, negative, and everything in between.

I believe emotions occur on a spectrum. Seemingly opposite emotions are merely different points along one continuum—just as hot and cold are merely expressions along the spectrum of temperature. Neither is inherently good nor inherently bad.

The same can be said for emotions. When they're extreme, particularly those that lean toward the negative, we start to get uncomfortable and judge ourselves. That can lead us to repress, ignore, or hide the negative emotions instead of letting them pass through us. When we don't allow ourselves to experience emotions fully, they can get stuck, resulting in bitterness or resentment.

The grids in this section are designed to keep your emotions moving through you so they don't get stuck. The grids can also help you connect emotionally to yourself, others, or the universe.

FORGIVENESS

Shape: Pentagram
Type: Releasing

People often misunderstand forgiveness. Many people believe forgiving someone means approving of bad behavior. But forgiveness is really about letting go of anger you hold toward another person. It's the realization that holding on to that negativity harms only you. Forgiveness is getting to a place where you no longer allow someone else's actions to control you. Interestingly, it usually begins with self-love. This grid can help foster forgiveness toward anyone, whether it's yourself or another person.

FOCUS STONE—ROSE QUARTZ

Rose quartz is the stone of unconditional love and forgiveness. It has a soft and yielding energy that brings you into a heart space where forgiveness begins. It can help you find a more compassionate place for yourself and others so you can begin to move forward.

DESIRE STONE—GREEN CALCITE

Green calcite can help absorb the excess energy of anger, hurt, and bitterness that often accompanies the need to forgive. It can also stimulate the heart and love energy necessary for forgiveness.

DIRECTIONAL STONE—CELESTITE

Celestite has an orthorhombic lattice structure (page 17), which makes it well suited for removing blockages. When you're really angry or bitter toward someone, those emotions tend to become sticky and get stuck inside of you. Celestite not only helps remove the energetic blockages caused by suppressed emotions but also helps remove criticism and judgment while facilitating clear and honest communication.

TIP TO EXPAND YOUR PRACTICE

This is a grid that may require daily resetting along with additional visualization work. In the presence of your grid, sit and close your eyes. Visualize the anger you feel toward whomever you need to forgive as dark clouds connecting you to them. Visualize yourself taking a pair of scissors and cutting those dark clouds until they dissipate. Visualize the other person surrounded in white light as you say aloud or in your mind, "I release you."

ALTERNATE CRYSTAL OPTIONS

Focus stone: Kunzite
Desire stone: Peridot
Directional stone: Sodalite

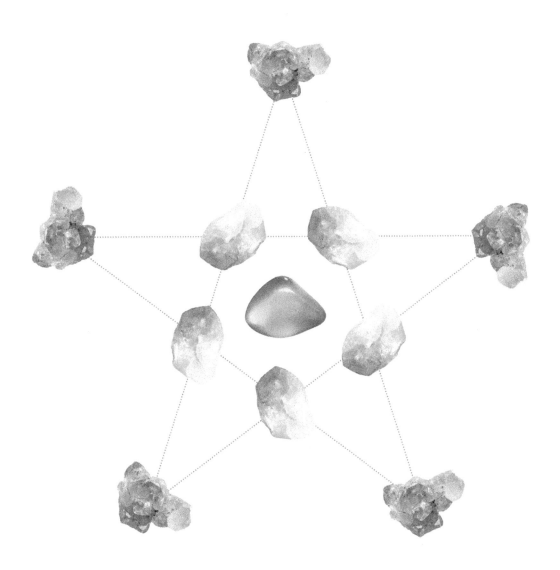

SELF-AWARENESS

Shape: Triquetra
Type: Magnifying

To live a life of purpose is to forge a deep connection with yourself. This means living in a state of self-awareness where you love all aspects of yourself unconditionally. This is no easy task. We often internalize negative messages about ourselves. We tend to hide our shortcomings in the shadows and refuse to acknowledge they exist. Self-awareness is the first step to self-love. Meet your shadows and shine a light on them so you can accept them as part of the harmonious whole that makes you.

FOCUS STONE—CARNELIAN

To gain self-awareness, listen to your internal dialogue instead of examining it. Carnelian can help you tune in to your gut feelings and give you the confidence to examine thoughts you have about yourself.

DESIRE STONE—YELLOW TIGER'S-EYE AND SMOKY QUARTZ

Yellow tiger's-eye is a stone of self-confidence and self-awareness. It allows you to recognize the soul that exists within you, beyond ego-identification. Smoky quartz can help turn negative thoughts about yourself into positive thoughts. Place tiger's-eye on the inside intersection of the lines of the triquetra and smoky quartz at the points.

DIRECTIONAL STONE—RAINBOW FLUORITE

Use rainbow fluorite to support self-love, remove criticism and judgment, and bring Divine guidance into your self-awareness. This will help you experience your true Divine nature. Place the rainbow fluorite in a ring around the outside of the triquetra.

TIP TO EXPAND YOUR PRACTICE

Shadow work can help you recognize, accept, and integrate those parts of yourself you hide from the rest of the world. Lie on the floor next to your grid. Close your eyes and visualize the negative things you see about yourself as dark shadows filling your body. Visualize a light flowing from the grid into your body, causing the shadows to break up and dissipate into the universe.

ALTERNATE CRYSTAL OPTIONS

Focus stone: Amber
Desire stone: Pyrite
Directional stone: Celestite

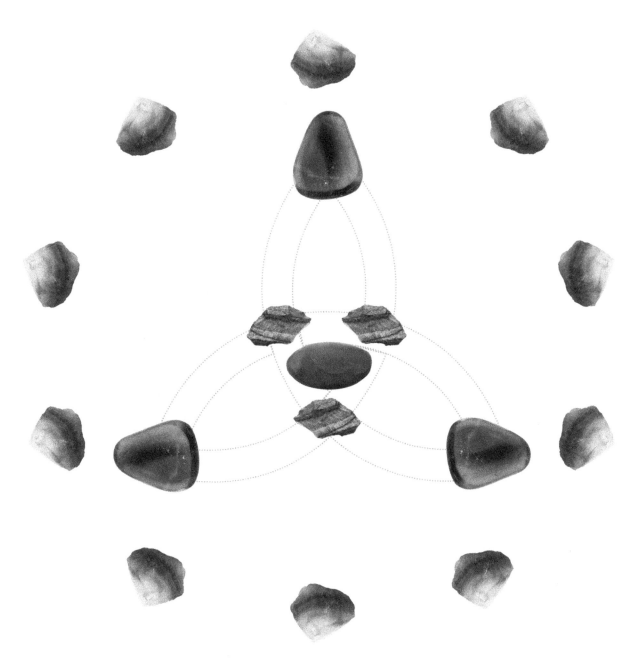

SELF-LOVE

Shape: *Lotus*
Type: *Strengthening*

There's a saying that you can't love another until you learn to love yourself. Learning to genuinely and unconditionally love yourself is much harder than it ought to be. This grid is designed to help remove blocks to self-love and strengthen your ability to love yourself.

FOCUS STONE—PERIDOT

With its focus on the heart center, peridot is a stone of self-love. It can also help you forgive yourself for anything you're holding on to and remove blockages to loving yourself, including releasing negative messages you've received about yourself.

DESIRE STONE—RAINBOW FLUORITE

With its multitude of colors, rainbow fluorite can help strengthen many aspects involved in self-love. Its yellow colors strengthen personal power and self-esteem, shades of pink amplify love, blue reduces judgment and criticism, and purple connects you to your Divine nature.

DIRECTIONAL STONE—ROSE QUARTZ

Rose quartz as your perimeter stone brings the energy of peace and unconditional love to this grid. It can help you love yourself, shadows and all, allowing you to integrate those things you see as negative into the positive whole that makes up your Divine essence.

TIP TO EXPAND YOUR PRACTICE

Write affirmations of self-love on pieces of paper. Try to come up with several positive statements about loving yourself and include why you love yourself. As you lay the grid, read each affirmation aloud, then place one under each crystal.

ALTERNATE CRYSTAL OPTIONS

Focus stone: Green calcite
Desire stone: Ametrine
Directional stone: Kunzite

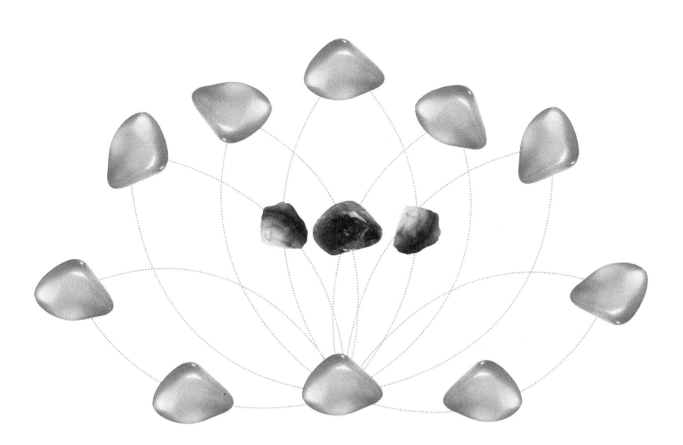

UNCONDITIONAL LOVE

Shape: *Tibetan Knot*
Type: *Strengthening*

The nature of the universe is unconditional love. Before we are embodied as human beings, we come from a place of unconditional love, and we return to it after we die. However, we often feel disconnected from this energy, unable to receive and give unconditional love. This grid can help strengthen universal love and remind us of who we truly are.

FOCUS STONE—ROSE QUARTZ

Rose quartz shows up in almost every love grid I create in some way or another because it is so deeply tied to unconditional love. This crystal carries the loving energy of the universe within it, providing the energy of love to all who work with it. It's the perfect focus stone for an unconditional love grid.

DESIRE STONE—MOONSTONE

Moonstone flashes with every color of the rainbow, and as it does, it draws in Source energy. The essential nature of Source energy is unconditional love. The flashes of color in the moonstone draw the unconditional love from the universe and distribute it throughout your physical being, filling you entirely with Source energy.

DIRECTIONAL STONE—CLEAR QUARTZ

Clear quartz in this grid acts as a signal amplifier. It pulls the love energy from the grid and from the universe and amplifies it in the space where the grid is placed. You can use any form of clear quartz here. You don't need to use points, but if you have them, place the terminated ends pointing toward the grid. This pulls the energy of love from the universe and infuses it into the grid.

TIP TO EXPAND YOUR PRACTICE

Adding spiral shapes to your grid can represent the outflow and growth of love. Add nautilus shells, snail shells, or sunflowers beside the grid or incorporate them among the crystals. Or, if you have ammonite fossils—spiral-shaped sea creatures similar to a nautilus—you can add these instead. The spiral shapes keep the energy of universal love ever opening and expanding.

ALTERNATE CRYSTAL OPTIONS

Focus stone: Morganite
Desire stone: Labradorite or opal
Directional stone: Selenite

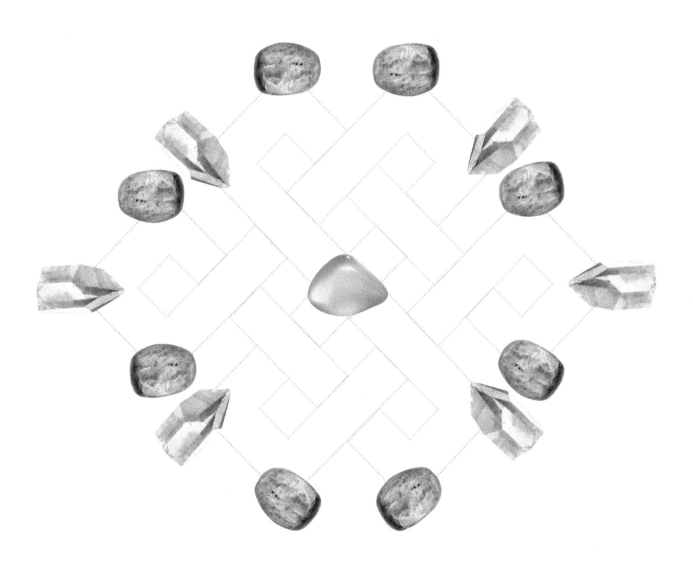

ROMANTIC LOVE

Shape: Vesica Piscis
Type: Magnetizing

If you'd like to attract a romantic partner or strengthen your current romantic relationship, this grid is right for you. It's not a magic bullet: If you're in a relationship that doesn't serve your greatest good, or you're trying to attract a specific person who isn't the right person for you, you'll be fighting an uphill battle. But this grid can be powerful when you combine it with the intention to be in a partnership that serves the highest good for both partners.

FOCUS STONE—PERIDOT

Peridot is an excellent stone for attracting romantic love. It vibrates with the energy of partnership, and it can help strengthen or attract soul mate relationships. Associated with the heart chakra, peridot can strengthen or attract romantic love.

DESIRE STONE—GARNET

Add red garnet to this grid to bring passion into the relationship or to help sustain passion in an existing relationship. The color red not only ignites passion but also helps you create appropriate boundaries so you don't become so enmeshed in the relationship that you lose yourself.

DIRECTIONAL STONE—LABRADORITE

Labradorite connects you to Divine guidance, which can help you recognize and identify the appropriate partner. It also fosters integrity, which is essential in relationships, and it facilitates communication between partners while removing criticism and judgment.

TIP TO EXPAND YOUR PRACTICE

Roses and jasmine are both flowers related to romantic love. Either diffuse one of these essential oils where you place your grid or add a ring of roses and/or jasmine around the outside of the grid to draw in more love energy.

ALTERNATE CRYSTAL OPTIONS

Focus stone: Emerald or ruby in fuchsite
Desire stone: Hematoid quartz
Directional stone: Rainbow fluorite or moonstone

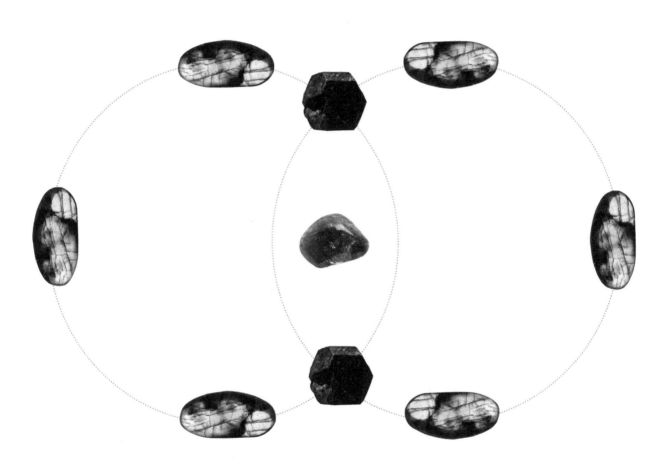

COMPASSION

Shape: *Triangle*
Type: *Expressing*

Compassion for self and others is the cornerstone of unconditional love and human connection. It allows us to truly connect with others and understand that the path they are walking is as important as ours. Compassion also prompts us to take loving action to alleviate suffering. Truly loving relationships are always based in compassion.

FOCUS STONE—ROSE QUARTZ

The gentle energy of rose quartz facilitates an opening of the heart, which is where compassion begins. It carries within it the loving and compassionate energy of the entire universe. It can also help foster acceptance and kindness, which are elements of compassion.

DESIRE STONE—CARNELIAN

Carnelian helps you act on your compassion by prompting you to reach out with kindness and care when you see another struggling.

DIRECTIONAL STONE—CELESTITE

Place a simple celestite ring around your triangle as the outer layer. Celestite removes criticism and judgment, and it also helps you communicate your compassion to others through your words and actions.

TIP TO EXPAND YOUR PRACTICE

Add affirmations to your practice such as "I am compassionate to the needs of others" and "I experience and receive compassion freely." Repeat them during meditation or as you drift off to sleep.

ALTERNATE CRYSTAL OPTIONS

Focus stone: Morganite
Desire stone: Amber
Directional stone: Blue lace agate

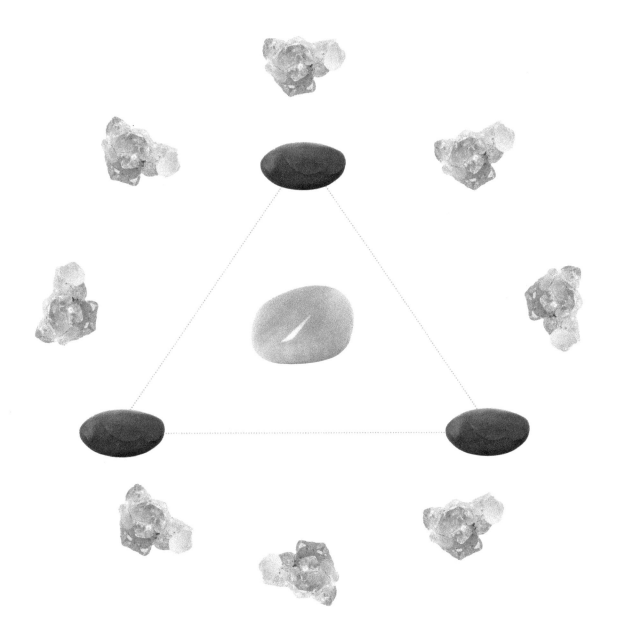

JOY

Shape: Sunburst
Type: Strengthening

We could all use a little more joy in our lives, yet many people don't make happiness or joy a priority. You can choose joy by staying focused on the present, engaging in activities you love, spending time with people you love, and seeking human connection.

FOCUS STONE—AMBER

Amber has a warm, vibrant, and inviting energy that sparks joy. Choose a sunny-colored piece as the focus stone to bring joy to your crystal grid.

DESIRE STONE—CARNELIAN AND CITRINE

For your desire stones, choose sunny-colored carnelian and citrine and create a circle around the focus stone by alternating the two crystals. Both of these stones attract joy with their vibrant shades and happy energy.

DIRECTIONAL STONE—CLEAR QUARTZ

Finally, make the sunburst layer clear quartz stones. Points are good here if you have them. Position them with the flat ends toward the grid and the pointed ends facing out into the universe to amplify the joy the grid sends into the spaces you occupy.

TIP TO EXPAND YOUR PRACTICE

This grid tends to be energizing, so be sure to place it somewhere other than your bedroom—otherwise you may struggle to sleep. Add the sunny scent of orange or lemon where you set it up by diffusing lemon or orange essential oil. Sit in the space with the grid and aromas and visualize things that bring you joy for five to ten minutes each day.

ALTERNATE CRYSTAL OPTIONS

Focus stone: Sunstone
Desire stone: Pyrite
Directional stone: Smoky quartz

ENTHUSIASM

Shape: Triskelion
Type: Energizing

I've always been blessed with an abundance of enthusiasm: think Tigger from Winnie-the-Pooh, but in the form of a woman. Enthusiasm can drive motivation, fuel passion, and enhance curiosity. It allows you to live in the moment and seek the experiences that bring you joy and serve your greatest good. If you're in a rut, it's hard to find enthusiasm, so this grid helps you both break free and move forward with ardor.

FOCUS STONE—AMETRINE

Ametrine, which is a combination of amethyst and citrine in a single stone, can help increase your enthusiasm and energy. It also connects Divine inspiration to personal will, which can help generate more excitement and enthusiasm.

DESIRE STONE—CELESTITE

With its orthorhombic lattice structure (page 17), celestite can help break up energy blockages that have you stuck in a rut. Celestite also removes judgment and criticism, which can block the energy of enthusiasm, and it facilitates communication, which allows you to act on your excitement.

DIRECTIONAL STONE—GARNET

Red garnet can help spark passion, which is an essential component of enthusiasm. It's also grounding, so it can help pull enthusiastic energy from a higher source and ground it in your physical presence.

TIP TO EXPAND YOUR PRACTICE

Choose a piece of music that excites and energizes you, something that fires you up and gets you going. Sit on the floor near your grid, close your eyes, and play your energizing song as you visualize that which you would like to be enthusiastic about.

ALTERNATE CRYSTAL OPTIONS

Focus stone: Amethyst
Desire stone: Blue lace agate
Directional stone: Hematoid quartz or ruby

RELEASING ANGER AND BITTERNESS

Shape: Triquetra
Type: Releasing

Anger is a natural part of the human experience. There's nothing wrong with the emotion of anger, because it serves a valuable purpose in our lives. However, we need to experience anger fully and allow it to pass through us, or it will become stuck and devolve into the destructive energy of bitterness, which can do lasting harm.

FOCUS STONE—GREEN CALCITE

Because it is an opaque stone, green calcite can absorb excess anger so it doesn't overpower you. Its warm green nature helps to balance and calm the heart chakra, which becomes overactive when you are angry.

DESIRE STONE—PERIDOT

Peridot amplifies love and promotes forgiveness—both important factors in releasing anger and relinquishing bitterness. The clear green color also helps provide the clarity you need to realize that your anger isn't serving your highest good, the object of your anger, or the universe as a whole.

DIRECTIONAL STONE—SMOKY QUARTZ

Making a perimeter of smoky quartz stones can help transmute the negative energy of anger and bitterness, first by allowing you to fully express and experience it, then by converting that negative energy into positive energy.

TIP TO EXPAND YOUR PRACTICE

If you're especially angry or feel controlled by anger, you'll need to reset this grid every day or two. Make sure to cleanse the crystals before resetting it. As you set the grid, place pink Himalayan salt crystals, which you can get at the grocery store, around the perimeter to absorb any excess anger before removing the crystals and then cleansing and resetting them.

ALTERNATE CRYSTAL OPTIONS

Focus stone: Malachite
Desire stone: Rose quartz
Directional stone: Black tourmaline

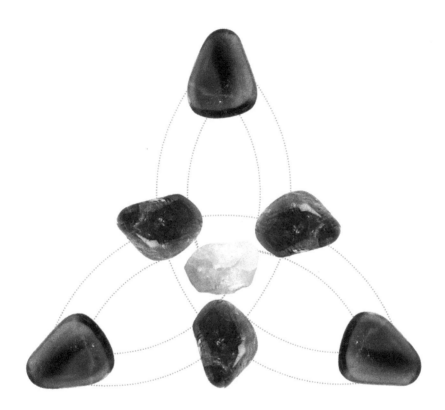

LETTING GO

Shape: Om
Type: Releasing

This grid is really more intuitive than structured. Use the Om shape as the basis for your grid, and then place the suggested stones along that shape. This grid has no focus, desire, or directional stones. The shape of Om and its energy can help connect you to the greater power of the universe, enabling you to let go of things that no longer serve you.

FIRST CRYSTAL—CITRINE

Use citrine to release emotional baggage. You can use one or as many pieces of citrine as you like in the shape of the Om grid.

SECOND CRYSTAL—BLUE LACE AGATE

Blue lace agate brings peace, and it helps you release judgment and criticism, which are all essential for letting go. Use as many pieces of blue lace agate as you deem appropriate or necessary.

THIRD CRYSTAL—ROSE QUARTZ

Rose quartz brings unconditional love to your Om grid. Use as many pieces as you need.

FOURTH CRYSTAL—RAINBOW FLUORITE

Rainbow fluorite connects all of your chakras, balancing the energy and allowing it to flow freely through you to remove any blockages.

FIFTH CRYSTAL—SELENITE

Finally, add selenite to bring Divine energy and guidance to your grid so you can see which things you need to release.

TIP TO EXPAND YOUR PRACTICE

Be very mindful as you set your grid. Place each stone with intention, and as you do, invoke the sound of Om aloud by chanting. This will draw the universal energy to your grid to help facilitate letting go.

ALTERNATE CRYSTAL OPTIONS

First stone: Pyrite
Second stone: Celestite
Third stone: Kunzite
Fourth stone: Labradorite
Fifth stone: Clear quartz

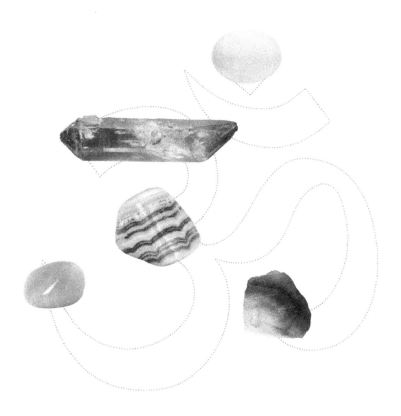

CHAPTER 9

Strengthen Your Spirituality

I BELIEVE WE ALL have a spiritual path to walk in this life. We come into each incarnation, become embodied, and have specific things we'd like to explore, learn, do, be, and accomplish, as well as issues we want to overcome. This is called our karmic imprint, and every soul has one. Throughout lifetimes of embodiment, we seek to experience ourselves as everything that ever was, is, or will be as we move closer to returning to the Source energy from which we came.

There is no "right" or "wrong" type of spirituality, just as there is no "right" or "wrong" spiritual journey. There's only your path. How you choose to walk it is entirely up to you. However, along the way, we do receive guidance from our higher selves, our spirit guides, the spirits of loved ones who have died, and even from Source energy itself. The grids in this chapter are designed to help you tune in to the spiritual, find guidance from your higher self and others, and continue walking the spiritual path that's right for you.

INNER PEACE

Shape: Star of David
Type: Soothing and Calming

Generations of humans have sought inner peace, a state of calm centeredness. In today's world, it's essential to achieve a state of serenity in spite of the drama swirling around in your outer environment. Once you find this peaceful place within yourself, return to it anytime you need to soothe anxiety, find clarity, or simply step away from the stresses and pressures of life.

FOCUS STONE—BLUE LACE AGATE

With its multiple shades of calming blue, blue lace agate eases stress and anxiety and radiates peaceful energy. It can also help remove roadblocks to peace, such as judgment and criticism, and it can facilitate acting and speaking with integrity, which is also essential for finding peace.

DESIRE STONE—MOONSTONE

Moonstone helps create inner peace and facilitate calm feelings. It also connects you to a higher power and Divine guidance. Knowing that connection is there, and that you can return to it anytime you wish, can also help you remain in a tranquil state—no matter what is going on around you.

DIRECTIONAL STONE—LABRADORITE

Labradorite's flashes of color and calming blue-gray tones support higher connection, inner peace, truth, and integrity.

TIP TO EXPAND YOUR PRACTICE

Meditate for five to ten minutes each day in the presence of your grid. Sit near the grid either on the floor or with your feet flat on the floor and look at it with a soft gaze. As you do, repeat the mantra "Om shanti shanti shanti," which means "Om peace peace peace."

ALTERNATE CRYSTAL OPTIONS

Focus stone: Celestite
Desire stone: Selenite
Directional stone: Rainbow fluorite

DIVINE DREAMING

Shape: Circle
Type: Connecting

I'm a big believer in the power of universal connection through dreams. Many of my spiritual inspirations and insights have come while I sleep. When my mind is calm, my higher self and spirit guides are better able to reach me. This grid can help you have inspired dreams and remember their content so you can carry over any insights into your waking life.

FOCUS STONE—AMETHYST

Amethyst has many qualities that can help with Divine dreams. First, it is the stone of dreams; it facilitates deeper sleep, guidance dreams, and dream recall. Likewise, it helps connect you to guidance from your spirit guides, making it ideal for Divine dreaming.

DESIRE STONE—SELENITE

Selenite is a stone of Divine guidance and connects you to Source energy. It also can help improve clarity, which can help you understand the messages you receive in your dreams. Selenite is also calming, so it won't interrupt your sleep if you set up the grid near your bed.

DIRECTIONAL STONE—SNOWFLAKE OBSIDIAN

Snowflake obsidian connects you to higher energy, and it helps you to ground Source energy in the physical. In other words, it helps you bring the content of your spiritual dreams into your waking life so you can walk a more spiritual path.

TIP TO EXPAND YOUR PRACTICE

Place this grid in your bedroom. Reset it about once a week. Each night as you go to sleep, focus on your grid for a moment and state your intention to the universe aloud or in your head. Then say, "Tell me what I need to know." When you wake up from a dream, immediately record a few details in a journal so you can better remember it when you are fully awake.

ALTERNATE CRYSTAL OPTIONS

Focus stone: Lepidolite
Desire stone: Moonstone
Directional stone: Smoky quartz

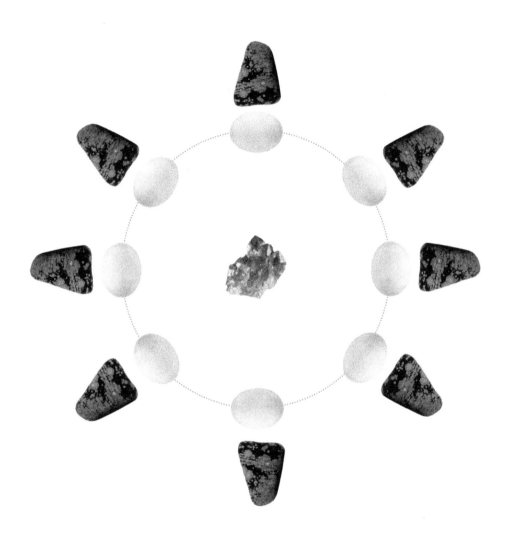

CONNECTION TO THE DIVINE

Shape: Tree of Life
Type: Balancing and Energizing

We are all connected to the Divine every moment of every day, whether we realize it or not. Unless we are highly tuned in, we tend to only recognize this in our quietest or most introspective moments, such as during meditation. This grid can help you maintain awareness of your connection to the Divine and call on it whenever you need.

FOCUS STONE—SNOWFLAKE OBSIDIAN

Snowflake obsidian carries energy from the crown to the root chakra, moving through each of your energy centers along the way. As the energy travels, it brings messages from higher planes. In other words, your higher guidance and Source energy sends it throughout your entire being. Place the snowflake obsidian in the number 6 and number 9 spots (page 55) on the Tree of Life as your focus stone.

DESIRE STONE—LABRADORITE

With its flashes of deep blues and purples, labradorite calls in the energy of the Divine. It opens your eyes and ears and allows you to see and hear guidance while helping you choose to live your truth with integrity. Place the labradorite pieces in each of the remaining circles on the Tree of Life grid.

DIRECTIONAL STONE—CLEAR QUARTZ

Surround your Tree of Life grid with a circle of clear quartz stones in any shape. The clear quartz provides clarity and discernment to help you recognize Divine messages, and it also amplifies the messages so you can hear them more clearly.

TIP TO EXPAND YOUR PRACTICE

Meditate with your grid for five to ten minutes each day. Keep a journal of the insights that come to you during your meditation. At the end of each week, go through and meditate on your insights as you reset the grid, giving thanks to the universe for sharing its energy and inspiration with you.

ALTERNATE CRYSTAL OPTIONS

Focus stone: Moonstone
Desire stone: Aquamarine or amethyst
Directional stone: Selenite

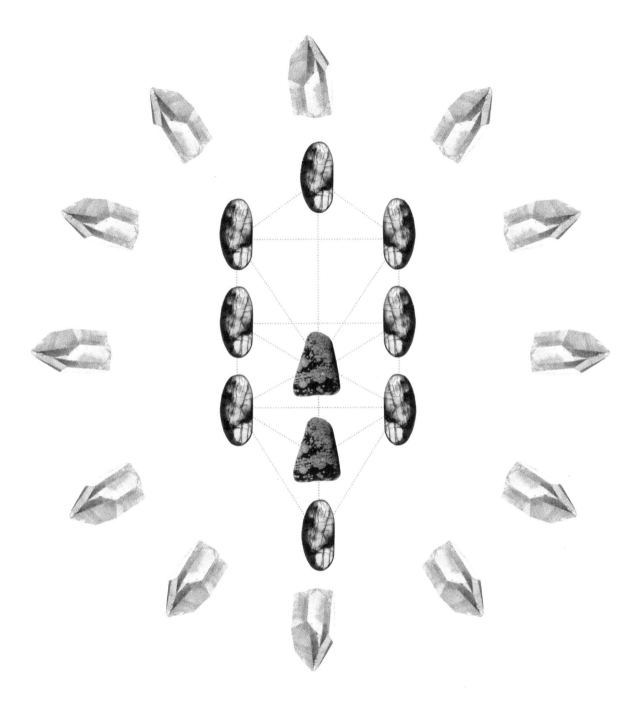

SPIRIT GUIDE COMMUNICATION

Shape: Lotus
Type: Connecting

Your spirit guides are conscious beings who constantly communicate with you. Their guidance typically comes in the form of what feels like intuition, random thoughts, hunches, insights, inspiration, or feelings. Guidance can also come in dreams and meditation. This grid will prompt you to be more open to spirit guide communication so that these wise counselors can help you as you travel your spiritual path.

FOCUS STONE—RAINBOW FLUORITE

With its balance of colors ranging from yellow to deep purple, rainbow fluorite pulls messages from your spirit guides in through your third eye and grounds them in your awareness. It can also help you recognize guidance and discern it from ego-driven thoughts or subconscious beliefs.

DESIRE STONE—MOONSTONE

Moonstone connects you to a higher power and serves as an amplifier to strengthen your reception to messages from spirit guides. It can also help you gain clarity so you better understand the intent behind the messages you receive and integrate them into your life.

DIRECTIONAL STONE—LABRADORITE

Labradorite both connects you to the energy of your guides and removes criticism and judgment that may block your reception of these messages. It strengthens intuitive third-eye reception and also facilitates living your truth, which your spirit guides encourage you to do.

TIP TO EXPAND YOUR PRACTICE

Spirals and items that represent spirals, such as snail or conch shells or sunflowers, allow energy to continuously expand outward. Place them in a circle around the grid to clarify your intent.

ALTERNATE CRYSTAL OPTIONS

Focus stone: Amethyst
Desire stone: Selenite
Directional stone: Blue lace agate or sodalite

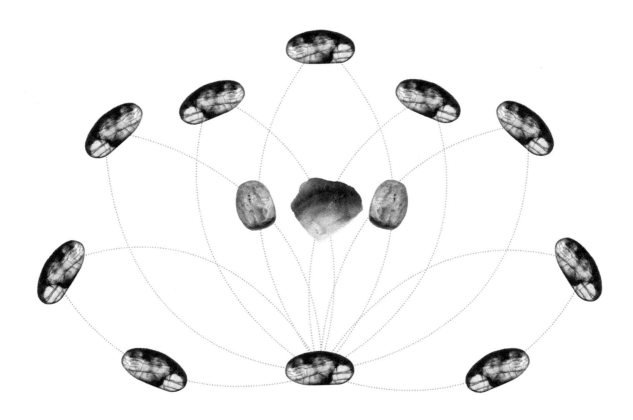

AURA CLEANSING

Shape: Yin-yang
Type: Cleansing and Balancing

Your aura is the field of energy surrounding you. It is one way the energy of your body connects to the energy of the universe. Your aura changes color depending on your mood and emotional state, spiritual learning, and other factors and feelings. Cleansing your aura can help remove any negative energy that it contains and replace it with positive energy.

FOCUS STONE—CHALCEDONY

You'll use two pieces of chalcedony in this grid—one in each of the inner circles of the yin-yang symbol. Chalcedony is a harmonizing and balancing crystal. As the focus stone of the grid, it sends the intent that you would like your aura balanced and harmonized.

DESIRE STONE—SELENITE

Selenite is a master cleansing crystal. It cleanses and purifies energy in all of your subtle (energetic) anatomy, including your aura, chakras, and meridians. Place the selenite at the perimeter of the circle on the yin-yang symbol to purify and cleanse your aura energy.

DIRECTIONAL STONE—SMOKY QUARTZ

Place an additional ring of smoky quartz around the outside of the yin-yang sign. This will turn any negative energy in your aura into positive energy while also balancing and grounding the energy throughout your physical being.

TIP TO EXPAND YOUR PRACTICE

As you set your grid, light a piece of palo santo or sage incense. Burning these items releases purifying smoke that cleanses energy. Sit near the burning incense and direct the smoke over and around you by fanning it with your hands or a feather. This will further cleanse your aura.

ALTERNATE CRYSTAL OPTIONS

Focus stone: Celestite
Desire stone: Clear quartz or moonstone
Directional stone: Black tourmaline

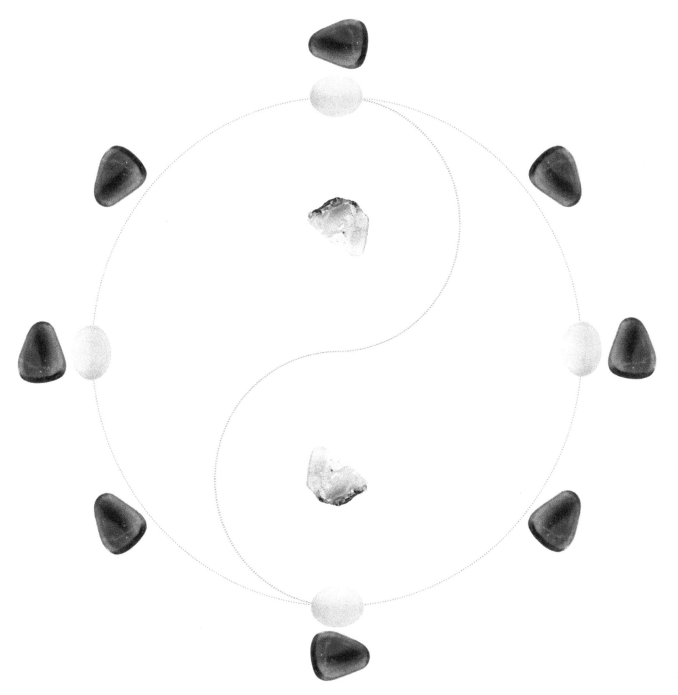

GROUNDING

Shape: *Pentagram*
Type: *Grounding*

Grounding allows you to remain connected to your physical self even as you work with your spiritual self and seek guidance. It allows you to bring spirituality into the physical world and also connects you to Gaia, or Mother Earth, who helps sustain and support the human race.

FOCUS STONE—CLEAR QUARTZ

Clear quartz stimulates and opens your crown chakra and connects you to the Divine. It is the focus stone of a grounding grid because the grid directs energy from the crown chakra all the way to the root chakra and into the earth.

DESIRE STONE—SNOWFLAKE OBSIDIAN

Snowflake obsidian takes the Divine energy from the clear quartz and pulls it down through each of your chakras and into your root chakra, where it awaits grounding. It brings Divine energy into your body and directs it throughout your being.

DIRECTIONAL STONE—BLACK TOURMALINE

Finally, black tourmaline ties the energy together, pulling it from your root chakra and grounding it in the earth. Once grounded, this energy is more easily applied to your daily life.

TIP TO EXPAND YOUR PRACTICE

Arrange your grid somewhere on the ground and sit next to it. Visualize roots growing from your root chakra and expanding down to the center of the earth. See the roots wrap around the center of the earth and visualize pink Earth energy moving up the roots and entering your core.

ALTERNATE CRYSTAL OPTIONS

Focus stone: Selenite
Desire stone: Moonstone
Directional stone: Garnet

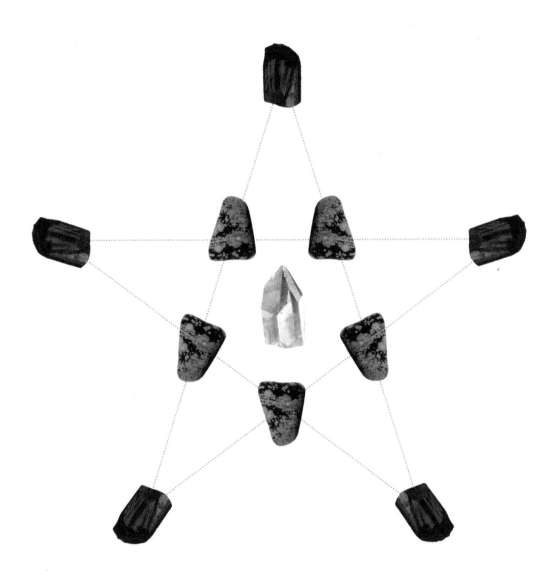

YOUR UNFOLDING SPIRITUAL PATH

Shape: *Tree of Life*
Type: *Harmonizing and Balancing*

This grid is meant to remove any blocks you may encounter on your spiritual path and provide balanced and harmonizing energy. It's more varied than others, and it has no focus, desire, or directional stones. The numbered positions for the stones are shown on page 55.

1—MOONSTONE

Moonstone stimulates your crown chakra and connects you to Source energy.

2 & 3—AMETHYST

Amethyst stimulates and balances your third eye chakra and connects you to your intuition and Divine guidance.

4 & 5—TURQUOISE

Turquoise balances and stimulates the throat chakra and connects you to Divine truth.

6—PERIDOT

Peridot balances the heart chakra and connects you to the energy of Divine love.

7 & 8—CITRINE

Citrine balances the solar plexus chakra and helps you understand how ego-identification affects you. It also helps improve self-esteem and personal will.

9—CARNELIAN

Carnelian balances your sacral chakra and connects you to Divine creativity.

10—GARNET

Garnet grounds the Divine in the physical and balances your root chakra.

TIP TO EXPAND YOUR PRACTICE

Place the crystals from the bottom up as you arrange your grid. In other words, start with number 10 and end with number 1. As you place each crystal, visualize its energy entering each chakra and flowing upward to create balance and harmony.

ALTERNATE CRYSTAL OPTIONS

1: Selenite
2 & 3: Lepidolite
4 & 5: Sodalite
6: Peridot
7 & 8: Pyrite
9: Amber
10: Black tourmaline

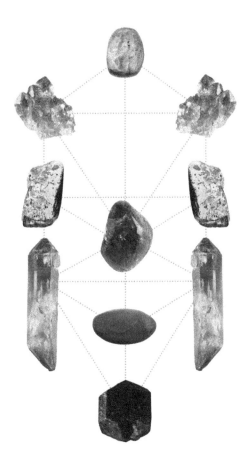

AWAKENING INTUITION

Shape: Om
Type: Expanding

This is another nontraditional grid layout in that it doesn't have focus, desire, or directional stones. Instead, you can lay the following stones anywhere you are guided to along the Om grid. Use this grid as a meditation. Hold each stone, contemplate it as you chant the syllable "om," and then lay the stone where your intuition guides you to.

FIRST CRYSTAL—AMETHYST

Amethyst supports intuition. It stimulates the third eye, invites you to connect with your higher self, reminds you to listen to higher guidance, and helps you receive messages that support your greatest good.

SECOND CRYSTAL—CHALCEDONY

Chalcedony stimulates the third eye and invites intuition. It also fine-tunes your receiver by opening your eyes, ears, and mind to intuitive messages that may arrive as a form of inspiration in the physical world. It also removes criticism and judgment while improving discernment.

THIRD CRYSTAL—MOONSTONE

Moonstone connects you to Divine inspiration while also directing it into your physical awareness so you can recognize inspiration and act on your intuition.

FOURTH CRYSTAL—RAINBOW FLUORITE

With its many colors, rainbow fluorite awakens intuition and also helps awaken your physical awareness of intuitive information in your body and mind.

TIP TO EXPAND YOUR PRACTICE

Intuition that goes unacknowledged often gets quieter and quieter until it goes away altogether. Keep a small notebook or journal with you, along with a pen. Whenever you have an intuitive thought, even if it flashes quickly, write a word or two in your notebook and take a moment to give thanks to the universe for providing intuitive insight.

ALTERNATE CRYSTAL OPTIONS

First crystal: Labradorite
Second crystal: Blue lace agate
Third crystal: Selenite
Fourth crystal: Snowflake obsidian

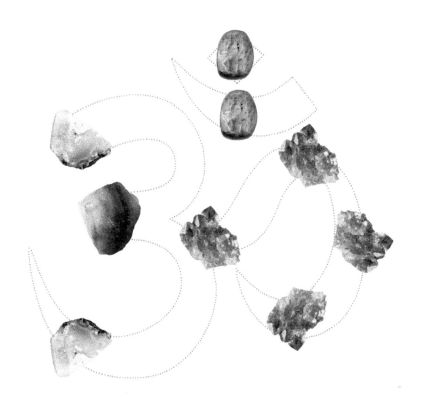

25 CRYSTALS FOR YOU

AMBER

Amber is not actually a crystal; it's petrified tree sap most frequently found on the Baltic coast. Still, it has healing properties primarily associated with its color and warm energy. It balances the energy of the sacral and solar plexus chakras, decreases inflammation, and can stimulate joy.

AMETHYST

Amethyst is a purple quartz variant with a hexagonal lattice structure. Its energy affects the third eye chakra and can help with sleep, dreaming, intuition, meditation, and communication with spirit guides. Amethyst is also known as "the sober stone" because it can help with addiction.

AMETRINE

Ametrine is another quartz variant with purple and yellow colors. It has a hexagonal lattice structure and balances the solar plexus and third eye chakras, connecting the energy of one to the other. It contains both amethyst and citrine and can replace either of these crystals in energy work.

BLACK TOURMALINE

Black tourmaline has a hexagonal lattice structure that balances the root chakra. It is one of the most grounding and protective crystals available. It absorbs negative energy and converts it into positive energy. It also creates a protective perimeter in grids to keep negative energy from reaching the other stones.

BLUE LACE AGATE

Another crystal with a hexagonal lattice structure, blue lace agate balances and energizes the throat chakra. It can soothe anxiety, promote creative expression, remove judgment and criticism, and help you live in truth and integrity. It is easily identifiable by its multiple shades of primarily light blue banding.

CARNELIAN

Carnelian is an orange to red-orange crystal with a hexagonal lattice structure. It balances the sacral chakra and also helps address sexuality issues, spurs creativity, strengthens personal will, and stimulates and promotes joy.

CELESTITE

Celestite is a heavenly blue-colored crystal with an orthorhombic lattice structure. It facilitates communication with spirit guides and a higher power. It can also balance both the third eye and throat chakras, remove criticism and judgment, and provide a calming, soothing energy to your grid.

CHALCEDONY

Chalcedony has a peaceful blue color and a hexagonal lattice structure. It balances both the third eye and throat chakras, facilitates peace, calms anxiety, soothes frayed nerves, and promotes truths shared with compassion.

CITRINE

Citrine is a yellow-colored quartz variant with a hexagonal lattice structure. Citrine can range in shade from pale yellow to deep orange-yellow or brownish-yellow. Darker citrines are typically man-made by heat-treating amethyst or smoky quartz. Citrine balances third chakra (solar plexus) energy. It promotes self-esteem and can help balance ego. It's also known as the prosperity crystal, stimulating wealth and abundance.

CLEAR QUARTZ

A crystal with a hexagonal lattice structure, clear quartz is considered the master healing crystal. It balances the crown chakra, amplifies the energy of all other crystals, can promote healing of body, mind, and spirit, facilitates Divine connection, and improves clarity.

GARNET (RED)

Garnet comes in many colors, although red is the most commonly known. For the grids in this book, we use the deep red version. Garnet has a cubic lattice structure and balances the root chakra. It's grounding, it promotes passion, and it can also help with issues associated with depression and absorbing negativity.

GREEN CALCITE

Green is only one color of calcite. You'll also find it in a rainbow of other shades, including blue, yellow, and orange. Calcite has a hexagonal lattice structure and a waxy sheen. The green variety is a soft green that balances the heart chakra. It helps absorb feelings of anger, bitterness, or rage, and it promotes romance, friendship, and unconditional love and forgiveness.

LABRADORITE

Labradorite is a blue-violet crystal with a triclinic lattice structure. The multicolored flashes of light that play throughout it are referred to as "labradorescence." Labradorite balances the throat and third eye chakras, facilitates communication with a higher power, and connects you to Divine guidance and Source energy. It also helps you to speak your truth with compassion and helps you surrender personal will to Divine will.

LEPIDOLITE

Lepidolite has a monoclinic lattice structure and ranges in color from rosy pink to deep purple. It balances the third eye chakra, and it can also promote sleep and dreaming, help you tune in to intuition, and connect Divine guidance to unconditional love.

MOONSTONE

Moonstone has a monoclinic lattice structure. It is milky white with flashes of colorful light that can provide balance among all the chakras, but especially the crown chakra. Moonstone helps ground Source energy in the physical, and its calming and soothing energy facilitates peaceful sleep and meaningful dreams.

PERIDOT

Peridot (also called olivine) is a clear green crystal with an orthorhombic lattice structure. It balances heart chakra energy, promotes forgiveness, and amplifies love. It can also be used to reduce feelings of anger, rage, and bitterness.

PYRITE

Pyrite has a cubic lattice structure and was referred to as "fool's gold" (due to its sparkling gold-like appearance) during the Gold

Rush. Its golden color makes it a good choice for grids intended to attract prosperity and wealth. Pyrite balances the solar plexus chakra and promotes self-esteem and self-confidence. It can also absorb excess ego-identification to help you walk a more spiritual path.

RAINBOW FLUORITE

Fluorite, a crystal with a cubic lattice structure, comes in multiple colors, including yellow, purple, pink, and green. Rainbow fluorite contains variegations of these colors blended together, which makes it a powerful stone. It can balance the energy of all the chakras, and it supports intuition, love, self-esteem, communication, and grounding.

ROSE QUARTZ

With its light pink to violet-pink color and hexagonal lattice structure, rose quartz is the go-to stone for any grids associated with the gentle universal energies of love, kindness, and compassion. It also balances the heart chakra and can help you find compassion for others.

SELENITE

Selenite is a milky white gypsum crystal with a monoclinic lattice structure. It is considered the master cleanser; you can use it to cleanse other crystals or to cleanse and balance the energy of the chakras, meridians, and auras. Selenite also connects you to Source energy and helps you gain clarity and listen to spiritual guidance.

SMOKY QUARTZ

Ranging in color from light gray to deep brown, smoky quartz has a hexagonal lattice structure. It balances the energy of the sacral and root chakras and can also help ground energy. It's a protective crystal that absorbs negativity, and it can transmute negative energy into positive.

SNOWFLAKE OBSIDIAN

Snowflake obsidian doesn't have a lattice structure because it's not actually a crystal, despite functioning as one energetically. Snowflake obsidian is a form of volcanic glass. It has a black background with white snowflake-like patterns on it. It ties together the crown and root chakras, drawing energy through all of your other chakras along the way. It can help ground Source energy in the physical and direct energy through your chakras and meridians.

SODALITE

This cubic crystal has a medium to deep blue color with white or lighter blue veins throughout. It balances the throat chakra and can absorb excess energy in that region. It promotes self-expression, creative expression, truth, and integrity, and it eliminates criticism and judgment.

TIGER'S-EYE (YELLOW)

Many people are surprised to learn that tiger's-eye comes in yellow, red, and blue. Yellow is the most common color available. It has a hexagonal lattice structure, and the yellow variety balances the energy of the solar plexus chakra. It's a crystal that helps you grow personal power without becoming too ego-identified, and it can strengthen willpower, promote self-esteem and self-worth, and support motivation in your career.

TURQUOISE

Turquoise has a triclinic lattice structure and is considered a master stone for physical healing. It can help with virtually every physical ailment, so it's always a good stone to have available for grids associated with physical health. It balances throat chakra energy, and it also promotes peace, wisdom, and living with integrity.

RESOURCES

WEBSITES

HealingCrystals.com—Resources about crystals and crystals for sale

CrystalPendulum.com—Crystal resources and articles

Minerals.net—A database with scientific and technical information about minerals

Myss.com—The website of author Caroline Myss, who offers great information about chakras

BOOKS

The Crystal Bible by Judy Hall

Crystals for Beginners by Karen Frazier

Crystals for Healing by Karen Frazier

The Crystal Alchemist by Karen Frazier

The Little Book of Energy Healing Techniques by Karen Frazier

Chakra Healing by Margarita Alcantara

The Subtle Body by Cyndi Dale

REFERENCES

"Autoimmune Disease List." *American Autoimmune Related Diseases Association*. www.aarda.org /diseaselist/.

Barrallo, Javier; Francisco González Quintial; and Santiago Sánchez-Beitia. "An Introduction to the Vesica Piscis, the Reuleaux Triangle and Related Geometric Constructions in Modern Architecture." Nexus Network Journal 17, no. 2 (July 2015): 671-84. doi:10.1007/s00004-015-0253-9.

Beer, Rober. *The Handbook of Tibetan Buddhist Symbols*. Boulder, CO: Shambhala Publications, 2003.

"Celtic Knots." *Celtic Life International*. September 24, 2019. https://celticlife.com/celtic-knots-2/.

Ferréol, Robert. "Archimedean Spiral." *Math Curve*. www.mathcurve.com/courbes2d.gb/archimede /archimede.shtml.

Ferréol, Robert. "Fibonacci Spiral/Golden Spiral." *Math Curve*. www.mathcurve.com/courbes2d.gb /logarithmic/spiraledor.shtml.

Ghose, Tia. "What Is the Fibonacci Sequence?" *LiveScience*. October 24, 2018. www.livescience .com/37470-fibonacci-sequence.html.

Kubzansky, Laura D.; Karestan C. Koenen; and Avron Spiro III, et al. "Prospective Study of Posttraumatic Stress Disorder Symptoms and Coronary Heart Disease in the Normative Aging Study." *Archives of General Psychiatry* 64, no. 1, (January 2007): 109-16. doi:10.1001 /archpsyc.64.1.109.

Liu, Yun-Zi; Yun-Xia Wang; and Chun-Lei Jiang. "Inflammation: The Common Pathway of Stress-Related Diseases." *Frontiers in Human Neuroscience* 11 (June 2017): 316. doi:10.3389 /fnhum.2017.00316.

Mark, Joshua J. "Great Pyramid of Giza." *Ancient History Encyclopedia*. December 19, 2016. Accessed July 31, 2019. www.ancient.eu/Great_Pyramid_of_Giza/.

Meisner, Gary. "Phi, Pi and the Great Pyramid of Egypt at Giza." August 18, 2012. www.goldennumber.net/phi-pi-great-pyramid-egypt/.

"Pentagram." *New World Encyclopedia*. Last modified February 4, 2019. www.newworldencyclopedia.org/entry/Pentagram.

Sakoulas, Thomas. "The Parthenon." ancient-greece.org/architecture/parthenon.html.

Schneiderman, Neil; Gail Ironson; and Scott D. Siegel, "Stress and Health: Psychological, Behavioral, and Biological Determinants." *Annual Review of Clinical Psychology 1, no. 1* (2005): 607-28. doi:10.1146/annurev.clinpsy.1.102803.144141.

Segal, Eliezer. "Kabbalah: The Ten Sefirot of the Kabbalah." *Jewish Virtual Library*. www.jewishvirtuallibrary.org/the-ten-sefirot-of-the-kabbalah.

Shnidman, Ronen. "The Star of David: More than Just a Symbol of the Jewish People or Nazi Persecution." *Haaretz*. May 1, 2019. www.haaretz.com/jewish/holocaust-remembrance-day/the-star-of-david-isn-t-just-jewish-1.5323219.

Silberberg, Naftali. "Star of David: The Mystical Significance—Kabbalistic Insights into the Star of David." *Chabad.org*. December 14, 2008. www.chabad.org/library/article_cdo/aid/788679/jewish/Star-of-David-The-Mystical-Significance.htm.

Smith, Donald A. "C-Reactive Protein Was a Moderate Predictor of Coronary Heart Disease." *ACP Journal Club* 141, *no. 2* (October 2004): 51. doi:10.7326/ACPJC-2004-141-2-051.

Thorp, Charley Linden. "Tibetan Sand Mandalas." *Ancient History Encyclopedia*. July 30, 2019. www.ancient.eu/article/1052/tibetan-sand-mandalas/.

Tsaousides, Theo. "Why Are We Scared of Public Speaking?" *Psychology Today*. November 27, 2017. www.psychologytoday.com/us/blog/smashing-the-brainblocks/201711/why-are-we-scared-public-speaking.

"Why Was Stonehenge Built?" *History*. April 10, 2013. Last modified September 1, 2018. www.history.com/news/why-was-stonehenge-built.

INDEX

ACKNOWLEDGMENTS

I am blessed to have a number of people in my life who support my writing. First, I'd like to thank my husband, Jim, and my sons, Tanner and Kevin. Having an author in the family, they put up with a lot. Many meals have been sacrificed when I've had my head buried in a project and forgotten to feed them. I'm grateful for their ongoing love and support.

I'm also thankful to my community of friends, who are my biggest cheerleaders, my most ardent students, and my most profound teachers. I'm always afraid I will forget someone, so I seldom name names, but I'm especially grateful to the members of the Vision Collective who have taught me, learned from me, and taught alongside me. Kristen Gray, Tristan David Luciotti, Luis Navarrete, Amy Castellano, Jason and Carolyn Masuoka, Sharon Lewis (AuroA), Mackenna Long, Seth Michael, Jyl Straub, and Kasci Lawrence, you inspire me, and I'm grateful.

As always, I'd like to thank Cheryl Knight-Wilson and Chad Wilson, who were the first to give me a forum for my energy healing and metaphysical writing. I continue to be a proud contributor to *Paranormal Underground* magazine, and I'm grateful for your ongoing support.

Finally, I'd like to thank the entire team at Callisto Media, including Carolyn Abate and the editing and art team, who make my work far better than it would be without them.

ABOUT THE AUTHOR

Karen Frazier is the author of books about metaphysics, crystal healing, energy healing, dream interpretation, and the paranormal. She has ghostwritten a number of books and written hundreds of articles about a variety of topics.

Karen is a columnist for *Paranormal Underground* magazine. She currently writes two columns for the magazine: "Metaphysics and Energy Healing" and "Dream Symbols and Interpretations." For more than seven years, Karen was also the cohost of Paranormal Underground Radio, and she formerly served as the managing editor of *Paranormal Underground*. She is also the paranormal and horoscopes editor for LoveToKnow.com, and she writes energy healing, crystal healing, feng shui, numerology, palmistry, psychic phenomena, paranormal, divination, and tarot articles for the site as well.

An intuitive energy healer who is an Usui Reiki Ryoho Master-Teacher (Shinpiden), Karen is also a Raku Kai Reiki Master, a Karuna Ki Reiki Master, a Crystal Reiki Master, and a certified animal Usui Reiki Ryoho practitioner, as well as an ordained minister for the International Metaphysical Ministry. She has studied extensively and taken professional-level courses in numerous energy, alternative healing, metaphysical, and divination techniques and concepts.

Karen holds a Bachelor of Metaphysical Science (B.MSc) and a Masters of Metaphysical Science (M.MSc) as well as a Ph.D. in Metaphysical Parapsychology from the University of Sedona. She is currently working on her doctoral dissertation focusing on sound as a source of spiritual healing in order to earn her Doctor of Divinity (DD) in Spiritual Healing from the University of Sedona.